My Sunday Best

What is it that makes one team a winner and the other an also-ran? As often as not, the detailed game plan, the special fire, the will to win was provided by one man—the coach. And though each of the men who have contributed to this unique collection would be the first to deny the suggestion, it is mostly the coach, rather than the superstar he directs, who shapes the ultimate destiny of the team.

Here are fourteen of professional football's top coaches describing the most exciting games they have ever coached—the pre-game planning, the build-up of tension as game-day approaches, the exhilarating or agonizing moments of success or failure, and finally the moment of victory when all the work and planning and practice are justified. These stories present a vivid panorama of the country's most popular spectator sport.

my sunday best

Compiled and Edited by
jack fleischer

Foreword by Pete Rozelle
Commissioner,
National Football League

TEMPO
BOOKS

GROSSET & DUNLAP
A NATIONAL GENERAL COMPANY
Publishers   *New York*

To the nation's high school football coaches—the unheralded men who first taught the fundamentals of the game to today's great players and coaches;

And to my beloved mother and father, who never understood sports but always encouraged my interest in them.

Library of Congress Catalog Card Number: 79-158749
ISBN: 0-448-05541-4

Tempo Books is registered in
  the U.S. Patent Office
Tempo Books edition 1972

Printed in the United States of America

Foreword

Reading *My Sunday Best* is at once an experience
in history and nostalgia, in excitement and action, and
in providing one more reminder that what football is
all about is the playing of the game. Too often recently
the trend has been to concentrate on the other facets,
the off-field developments, the non-competitive side
such as labor negotiations, court cases, and similar
matters. For each of these coaches to limit his career
to one memorable game is a great problem, for there
are exciting memorable things happening on the playing field every week and they have been throughout
the history of the NFL. I'm delighted for the extra
chance *My Sunday Best* gave me to get back to the
playing field.

PETE ROZELLE
Commissioner, National Football League

Contents

George Halas

1940 NFL Championship Game
Chicago 73, Washington 0

Professional football owes much of its success to George S. Halas, Sr., who helped organize the National Football League in 1921.

Halas was the first coach to hold daily practices; the first to study motion pictures of games; the first to bring the modern T formation to the pros.

As coach of the Chicago Bears for 39 years, he compiled the enviable record of 321 regular season victories while losing 142 games and tying 31. His Bears won world championships in 1921, 1933, 1940, 1941, 1946 and 1963.

His teams averaged approximately seven wins against three defeats, and in only six of his 39 seasons did any of his clubs fall under the .500 mark.

Two of his teams had perfect seasons, and seven lost only one game.

A member of the Professional Football Hall of Fame, Halas points proudly to the fact that

1

there are more former Bears players in the Hall of Fame than any other team. These include: Red Grange, Sid Luckman, Paddy Driscoll, Bulldog Turner, Bronko Nagurski, Joe Stydahar, George McAfee, Dan Fortmann, Ed Healey, George Trafton and Link Lyman.

Known affectionately as Papa Bear to his former players, Halas, a former University of Illinois football star, has been owner of the Bears since he organized the team in 1921. He retired as coach after the 1967 season but still remains active in the front office operation of the team.

In 1970, he was elected the first president of the National Football Conference.

As head coach of the Chicago Bears for 40 years, I had many memorable games, but when you limit it to my most memorable one, it can only be our 73-0 playoff victory over Sammy Baugh and the Washington Redskins for the 1940 world's professional championship.

A close second would have to be the 1934 title game which we lost, 30-13, to the New York Giants under quite unusual circumstances. I'll certainly never forget that contest, which became known as the "sneakers" or "rubber shoe" game.

It was played on December 9 under horrendous

weather conditions. A regular nor'easter was blowing; the temperature was nine degrees and the Polo Grounds was covered with a sheet of ice.

Bronko Nagurski's touchdown and Jack Manders' field goal offset Ken Strong's field goal to give us a 10-3 lead at half-time, but Coach Steve Owen outfitted the Giants in basketball shoes in the second half, and the sure footing enabled them to score four last-period touchdowns.

Ironically enough, I had remarked on the way out to the Polo Grounds that after all our careful preparations, we had overlooked one thing—tennis shoes. And that was the difference.

It ended an 18-game winning streak which still stands as a record in league play. The streak had started near the end of the 1933 season when we won our four last regularly scheduled games and then beat the Giants, 23-21, for the championship. In 1934, we won 13 in a row, including two victories over the Giants, before we lost to them in the playoffs.

We found little consolation in beating the Giants, 21-0, a month later in a post-season game in Los Angeles. Although we had defeated them three times, they were still the 1934 league champions.

I consider the 1934 Bears on par with my 1940 club which has been rated the best pro football team of all time by the National Academy of Sports Editors. In finishing the regular season undefeated, the '34 team led the league in rushing, total yards and scoring. They would have repeated as world champions, too, if they had worn sneakers.

There were a number of reasons why I selected our 73-0 victory on December 8, 1940, in Washington over the Redskins as my most memorable one. Of course, the score was the most striking reason.

To me, it was the greatest team effort in my entire career as a coach. Everybody wanted to play, and when they got into the game, every player was at peak form. No changes in the lineup had any effect at all on the overall performance of the team.

All 33 players on the squad saw action. Sid Luckman played only the first half. Bernie Masterson, Bob Snyder and Sollie Sherman alternated at quarterback in the second half, but it was impossible to hold the score down. Every man was in there to win and to contribute something to the winning. I can't recall any high scoring game where the distribution of touchdowns was so widespread. Ten different players scored our 11 touchdowns. Only Harry Clark scored twice.

The game resulted in the universal acceptance of the T formation which all teams now use. I well remember that Earle "Greasy" Neale, who was to become head coach of the Philadelphia Eagles in 1941, got the film of the game and charted every play, saying that any system good enough to score that many points was going to be good enough for him.

This game also avenged a 7-3 defeat at the hands of the Redskins just three weeks earlier. We thought that we were going to win on the final play of that game when Luckman passed from the Redskin six-yard line to Bill Osmanski in the end zone. It was a perfect strike that bounced off Bill's chest. There was a good reason why Bill had been unable to catch the pass. His hands had been pinned to his sides by Frank Filchock. The officials did not call interference despite our players' protests, and the game was over.

In post-game interviews, the Redskins called the Bears "cry-babies" while George Marshall, owner of the Redskins, made the tart observation that we were front runners and strictly a first-half ball club which folded when the going got tough.

The heart-breaking loss and the snide remarks combined to inspire the Bears to herculean efforts in preparing for the championship game. I don't think that the players needed any reminders, but on the Monday before the play-off, our dressing room walls were plastered with clippings detailing the Redskins' opinions of the Bears.

Hunk Anderson and Carl Brumbaugh were my only assistants in those days, so I brought in Clark Shaughnessy, head coach at Stanford, to give us a hand for the title game. Clark, who had taken the T formation to Stanford and had enjoyed a great season, was a wizard in analyzing game film. We ran and re-ran films of our loss to Washington. We determined why certain plays worked and why others failed. The players were shown their mistakes on film over and over again. Certain plays would be re-run 30 to 40 times at one sitting.

Each morning session would start with the

showing of the film. Then, there was practice on the field, followed by chalk talks, lectures, written examinations on individual assignments and more movies.

When we left Chicago for Washington by train, I never saw a squad of players so deadly serious. There was none of the card playing or joking or pranks or laughing that is part of the relaxation on a road trip. The players sat huddled in their seats, studying their notebooks.

Rarely have I used oratory to fire up a team before it takes the field for a game. In any event, it certainly was not necessary before this game. The squad was heated mentally to the maximum.

We reviewed our two offensive game plans just before the kick-off. Game plan No. 1 would be in effect if the Redskins used the same defense they had employed in our previous game. Our first four plays were designed to feel them out, but as it turned out, we found the answer after just two plays. They were using the same defense and game plan No. 2 was never needed.

As for our defensive plans, we were thoroughly familiar with the Washington offense, and since we had held them to seven points in our last meeting, we were satisfied that we had them defensed very well.

Our main concern, of course, was Baugh. With his quick release—his ability to get the ball off so fast —there was no value in rushing him. Our defensive ends would drop back to cover the flat. This strategy proved especially effective in the third peri-

6

od when we intercepted three passes and ran them back for touchdowns. In all, we picked off eight of their passes.

We received the opening kick-off, and Luckman immediately called a "feeler" play to test the Redskins' defense. Ken Kavanaugh, our left end, was placed 18 yards out on the flank, and the Washington right halfback followed him out. Ray Nolting, at left half, was sent in motion to the right, and the Redskins' linebacker trailed him.

That was all Luckman had to see. The Redskin defense had not changed. George McAfee took a short pitch from Luckman and bolted between right guard and tackle for eight yards.

Here is a diagram of that play:

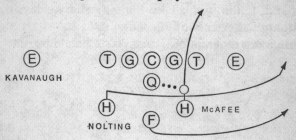

Then, on the next play, Kavanaugh again went wide, but McAfee went in motion to his left. Luckman made a reverse pivot and handed the ball to Osmanski on a run to the spread side. I remember later that Sid said: "Bill was really driving when I handed off. I knew he was going some place in a hurry."

7

That "some place" was 68 yards to a touchdown.

Actually, this play did not go according to plan. It originally called for a straight slant off left tackle, but when McAfee's block had not flattened the Redskin right end, Osmanski was afraid that the end would reach out and grab him so he made a dip towards the line and then ran wide around the end. Bill streaked away as George Musso blocked out the up-man in the secondary. Near the Redskin 35, Ed Justice and Jimmy Johnston started to close in on Bill, but neither saw George Wilson, who had cut across fast from his right end position.

As Justice started to tackle Osmanski, Wilson hit him with such force that the impact sent him into Johnston. Two men on one block! Osmanski went the rest of the way all by himself, and we had our first score after only 55 seconds.

Here is a diagram of Osmanski's touchdown run:

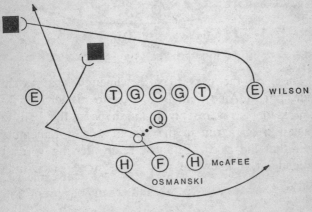

The Redskins came roaring back. Max Krause took the kick-off on his four and ran it back 56 yards before Osmanski tackled him on our 40 and prevented him from going all the way. Baugh moved the Redskins to the 25, but our defense held and Bob Masterson's 32-yard field-goal attempt failed.

We took over on our 20, and in 17 plays we went 80 yards, with Luckman sneaking over from the one-foot line for our second touchdown. Sid remained on the ground all the way during this drive. Our running game was doing the job, and wise quarterback that he was, Sid stayed with what was working.

A few minutes later, we took a 21-0 lead when Joe Maniaci raced 42 yards on a standard fullback-lateral play.

We missed two scoring opportunities in the second quarter, once when Ray McLean fumbled on the Redskins' 11 on a first down play and later, when Phil Martinovich failed on a 30-yard field-goal attempt.

Finally, near the end of the period, we were able to get on the scoreboard again. After Nolting intercepted a Filchock pass on our 34 and ran it back 10 yards, we moved to the Redskins' 30 on six ground plays. Then, on one of the few times we passed all day, Luckman hit Kavanaugh with a perfect toss in the corner of the end zone over the heads of Filchock and Andy Farkas.

The Redskins' most serious scoring threat came as time was running out in the half when they went 75 yards on eight pass plays to within one yard of our goal line. But Osmanski intercepted Baugh's pass on the final play of the half.

What do you tell a team in the dressing room at half-time when it has performed so magnificently and is leading 28-0? I simply told them: "Don't forget . . . the Redskins called us a first-half team apt to fold in the second half . . . don't forget that!"

The players let out a roar which more than convinced me of their readiness for the second half.

On the second play of the third period, Baugh's pass in the flat was intercepted by Hampton Pool, who ran it back 15 yards for the touchdown. It was our defensive plan against Baugh working to perfection.

Then, trailing 35-0, Baugh became desperate. On fourth and 20 from his own 34, he attempted a long pass which was incomplete. We took over deep in Redskin territory.

Nolting picked up 11 yards and then, on a quick opening play, he went over tackle, broke into the open, side-stepped Baugh and scored on a 23-yard run. Nolting was superb on these quick openers, and there hasn't been anyone better to this day.

Two more pass interceptions gave us a 54-0 lead by the time the third period ended. McAfee made a shoe string catch of a pass by Roy Zimmerman and went 34 yards, and Clyde Turner ran 21 yards after picking off another Zimmerman toss.

With a rookie quarterback, Sollie Sherman, running the team, we drove 58 yards on nine running plays for our ninth touchdown of the game. Harry Clark went the final 44 yards on a double reverse, a play that worked far more successfully than expected. But it was an afternoon when we could do nothing wrong.

In just a few minutes, the parade of touchdowns continued. A snap from center got away from Filchock, and Turner recovered for us on the Redskins' two. After Gary Famiglietti scored, the referee came over and asked us not to attempt the extra point with a kick. It seemed that we had kicked so many balls into the stands that only practice balls were left. So instead of trying the conversion by place-kicking, we passed and Sherman's completion to Maniaci made it 67-0, a new league record.

On the second play after the next kick-off, Maniaci intercepted a long Filchock pass—our eighth interception of the game—and returned 21 yards to the Redskins' 42. With Snyder now in at quarterback, we scored on 11 plays, Clark getting our eleventh and final touchdown on a plunge from the one.

The massacre was over. It had been impossible to hold the score down. The fierce competitive desires of the entire squad had been too great. Every element of offensive and defensive play had contributed to this historic game.

Earle (Greasy) Neale

1946 NFL Game
Philadelphia 28, Washington 24

Earle (Greasy) Neale was enshrined in Pro Football's Hall of Fame in 1969, but some 60 years before that, back in Parkersburg, West Virginia, he was already destined for immortality.

Neale not only was captain of his Parkersburg High School football team but he served as its coach as well and led the team to a state championship.

His fame continued as a college freshman at West Virginia Wesleyan in 1912. Before Wesleyan's big game against its deadly rival, West Virginia, a team it had never beaten, Greasy suggested a new play to his coach and then proceeded to lead his team to a 19–14 upset victory.

Later, his college coaching career at Marietta, West Virginia Wesleyan, Washington and Jefferson, Virginia, West Virginia and Yale was highlighted by the 1921 Washington and Jefferson team which went undefeated in 10 games and then held heavily favored California to a scoreless tie in the Rose Bowl.

Greasy entered the pro coaching ranks in 1941 at Philadelphia, and three years later he had the Eagles in second place. Then in 1947, his team won the eastern division title only to lose to the Chicago Cardinals, 28–21, in the NFL playoff game.

But it was a different story the next two years with the Eagles reigning as world champions by virtue of their 7–0 win over the Cardinals in 1948 and their 14–0 victory over the Los Angeles Rams in 1949. Those championship teams are regarded by many as being among the greatest in pro football history.

Neale, who was born November 5, 1891, in Parkersburg, lives in retirement in West Palm Beach, Florida.

It has been more than 20 years, but it is not difficult for me to remember my most memorable game as a pro coach. I had to look up some of the details, but I will never forget that day in Washington, D.C., when my Philadelphia Eagles were trailing Sammy Baugh and the Redskins, 24-0, in the third period, and we wound up winning, 28-24.

At that time, October 27, 1946, our victory was called the greatest comeback by any team in the history of the National Football League. I believe that game still stands today as the greatest comeback of all time.

We came to Washington with a 2-2 record, knowing that a defeat would just about eliminate us from the Eastern Division title We had started the season in great fashion, beating Los Angeles and Boston, but the next two weeks were disastrous ones as we lost to Green Bay and the Chicago Bears.

The Redskins were leading the Eastern Division with an undefeated record of three wins and a tie, and they needed a win against us to stay ahead of the New York Giants.

We all knew that Redskin coach Turk Edwards would have his team up for this game, and we worked hard all week, setting up defenses against Baugh's passes and planning some new offensive plays.

It didn't help our game plan when we learned that Steve Van Buren would be out of the line-up with an injury. Your running game has to be affected when you lose a great running back like Van Buren.

However, we were encouraged when on the second play of the game, Ernie Steele cracked the Redskin line and went for 43 yards. He would have gone all the way, but Dick Todd saved the touchdown by tackling Steele on the Washington 27-yard line.

We couldn't move the ball after that, and the Redskins took over. We looked good in holding

Washington on their first series of offensive plays, but when we got the ball again, we ran into trouble right away as Jack Jenkins intercepted a Tommy Thompson pass and ran 28 yards down the sidelines to the Eagle 18-yard line.

Washington moved on the ground to the two, from where Sal Rosato went over for the touchdown. Dick Poillon kicked the extra point, and Washington led, 7-0.

Not too much later in the first period, Wilbur Moore intercepted another Thompson pass on his own 40 and ran it back 30 yards to our 30-yard line. The Redskins could gain only one yard on three plays, and on fourth down, they were forced to settle for a field goal by Poillon from the 29. That made it, 10-0, Washington, and the first period ended that way.

We didn't look any better in the second period, but we did manage to keep the Redskins from scoring until late in the quarter. Then, Thompson had his third pass intercepted, this time by Clyde Ehrhardt, who grabbed the ball on the Eagle 45 and ran it back all the way to the seven. Rosato took it over from there, and Poillon added the extra point, making it Washington 17, Philadelphia 0.

There was only a minute and a half left when the Redskins kicked off to us on the 14. On the very first play, Allie Sherman, who was then in at quarterback, tried to hand off the ball, but there was all kinds of confusion in our backfield. I don't even know who was supposed to get the ball. All I remember was the ball was suddenly rolling towards the end zone, and Ted Lapka fell on it under the goal posts for another Redskin touchdown. After Poillon kicked the extra point, it was 24-0, Washington, and we were a pretty unhappy team as we left the field at half-time.

We were an unhappy lot but were far from discouraged. The three Washington touchdowns and field goal were all set up as the result of our mistakes, and not because the Redskins were so superior to our ball club.

We just couldn't get going in that first half. It seemed like everything we did went wrong. Working out of the T formation, we weren't able to run or pass. Our blocking was especially bad on our passes, and Thompson wasn't being given a chance. It was no wonder that he had three interceptions.

We weren't too much better during the early part of the third period as far as moving the ball was concerned. The Redskins backed us up to our own one-yard line mid-way in the period, and when Jim Youell returned our punt to our 25-yard line, it didn't look too encouraging for us.

But then we got our first break as Rudy Smeja recovered Poillon's fumble on the 30. We lost three yards on two plays from the T formation, so I signalled Thompson to go into a single-wing-back spread formation. This was the formation that the former Redskin coach Ray Flaherty had used so effectively.

I decided that we had to shift away from the T

because all three quarterbacks I had been using—Thompson, Zimmerman and Sherman—were under too much pressure from the Redskin line.

On third down and 13 yards to go, Thompson was now eight yards back with plenty of time to throw, and he hit Steele over the middle for 17 yards and a big first down.

On that particular play, Bosh Pritchard was supposed to go down five yards and then cut out, but he had kept right on going down the field. I told Thompson to run the same play again, but this time to tell Pritchard to go only five yards down.

Pritchard ran the pattern right, and Thompson hit him with an eight-yard pass. Bosh slipped a little after making the catch, and Moore, a great defensive back, rushed in to tackle him, but Pritchard side-stepped him and went all the way for our first touchdown. The play covered 56 yards. Augie Lio kicked the extra point, and we trailed 24-7, with about six minutes left to play in the third period.

About three minutes later, we had another chance when we recovered a Washington fumble on their 15. We went into the single-wing-back formation again. Thompson passed to Jack Ferrante for five, and an offside penalty against the Redskins put the ball on the five.

Steele hit the center of the line to the one-yard line. Mel Bleeker tried the same spot, but he was stopped cold. Thompson then pitched out to Steele, who raced around end for our second touchdown. Lio

17

again kicked the extra point, and we now trailed, 24-14.

In the fourth quarter, Thompson completely confused the Washington defense by shifting back and forth from the T to the single wing almost every other play. Starting from our own 35-yard line, Thompson passed most of the way to get us our third touchdown.

He hit Dick Humbert for 11 and Gil Steinke for 31. Steinke almost went all the way on that play, but Youel stopped him with a great tackle on the Redskin 19.

Thompson passed to Jim Castiglia for seven, and Steinke hit the middle for four and a first down on the eight-yard line. From the single wing, Thompson passed to Steinke on the five, and Gil broke away from a Redskin tackler to go across for the touchdown. Lio's extra point brought the score to 24-21 with just a little more than five minutes left.

We kicked off to the Redskins, hopeful of stopping them and getting another chance to score. With just under three minutes to play in the game, the Redskins had the ball on their own 40, with a fourth down coming up and one yard to go.

Baugh faced the decision of either punting and giving us another chance or going for the first down and then running out the clock. This is one of those calls that gives the Monday morning quarterbacks something to talk about the rest of the season.

Baugh apparently had confidence in Sal Rosata, who had shown good power in scoring two touchdowns in the first half, so he decided to go for the first down. But Ben Kish and Dick Humbert were right there when Rosato hit the line, and they stopped him cold.

We called a time out and Thompson came over to the sideline to talk with me. I told him to try 71 down and out to the sideline in order to bring in the Redskins' defensive back who was covering Ferrante, and to then try 71 long. On 71 down and out, Thompson overshot Ferrante, but on 71 long, the defensive back, whose name I don't recall, ran in to cover Ferrante again. This time, instead of cutting out, Ferrante just kept right on going down the field and when he turned at the goal line, he was all alone.

That was really a beautiful sight to see Ferrante standing there all by himself, and Thompson hit him with a perfect strike to put us ahead. Lio again kicked the extra point, making it 28-24.

There were now only about 90 seconds left in the game, but when a great passer like Sammy Baugh is in there against you, anything can happen.

We kicked off short to the 35-yard line so that none of the Washington fast deep men could get a chance for a long run back. Baugh went into the single-wing-back formation they had discarded three years before, and we had stolen from them. He picked up two first downs, and then on a long pass which could have won the game for them, Ernie Steele intercepted and that was the ball game.

And what a ball game to win! Nothing at all

worked from the T formation for more than half of the game, but once we shifted to the single wing and kept mixing it with the T, we were able to work our plays well.

This was really a team effort. It has to be when you are 24 points behind in the third quarter and you are able to beat a great quarterback like Sammy Baugh.

And without meaning to slight any of my other players, I can't help but say something about the play of Tommy Thompson. After having three of his passes intercepted and turned into scores in the first half, he performed magnificently from both the single wing and the T in the second half and wound up completing 18 out of 24 passes.

That was a memorable performance in my most memorable game as a pro coach.

Weeb Ewbank

*1958 NFL Championship Game
Baltimore 23, New York 17
and
1969 Super Bowl
New York 16, Baltimore 7*

Weeb Ewbank is the first coach to win world pro football championships in two leagues.

He won back-to-back titles in 1958 and 1959 as coach of the Baltimore Colts in the National Football League, and then, in 1969, his New York Jets of the American Football League conquered Baltimore in the Super Bowl. He was the first AFL coach to accomplish this feat.

Weeb is a graduate of Miami University of Ohio where he was a quarterback, captain of the baseball team and, in spite of his small stature, a member of the basketball team.

He began his football coaching career at his alma mater as an assistant coach and spent 14 years there. In 1943, he became a member of Paul Brown's staff at the Great

Lakes Naval Station, and after the war became backfield coach and head basketball coach at Brown University.

Weeb moved next to Washington University in St. Louis as its head football coach, and his two-year record of 14–4 was the best the school enjoyed in 30 years.

He became Paul Brown's line coach at Cleveland in 1949 and remained in that capacity with some of the Browns' greatest teams.

In 1954 when he was named Baltimore's head coach, Ewbank took a Baltimore team which was one of the worst in pro football and within six seasons produced two championship clubs. He performed similar coaching miracles with the New York Jets in five seasons after taking over the helm in 1963.

Weeb is a native of Richmond, Indiana.

It was just impossible for me to select one game as my most memorable one as a pro coach. It had to include two games, and I feel very fortunate to have been a part of two such great events.

How can I ever forget the National Football League championship play-off game in 1958 when the under-rated Baltimore Colt team I was then coaching defeated the New York Giants, 23-17, in a sudden-death overtime which is still considered by many as the greatest football game ever played?

And equally memorable to me was the Super Bowl game in 1969 when the New York Jets, a three-touchdown underdog, scored a 16-7 victory over my former Baltimore team to become the first American Football League representative to win the world's championship.

The win over the Giants was a great thrill for me because it was my first championship as a head coach. I had been involved in championship games before as an assistant coach for the Cleveland Browns, and those had been gratifying experiences, but Cleveland had been Paul Brown's team. Now, for the first time, a team of my own had gone all the way.

This championship was important to me, too, because it was a great team effort by some dedicated players, many of whom had been cast-offs from other clubs. The most famous cast-off, of course, was John Unitas, who was unable to make the Pittsburgh Steelers' squad and was playing sandlot ball at the time we picked him up just two years earlier.

The story about how we acquired John has been told many times, but it's worth repeating.

It all started when we received a letter about John from one of our fans in Pennsylvania. I always accuse John of having written it himself. In any event, the letter impressed me enough to check with his college coach, Frank Camp, of the University of Louisville.

23

Frank told me that he felt Unitas had fine possibilities and deserved another chance. One of our coaches, Herman Ball, told me that when John had tried out with Pittsburgh, he was competing against two experienced quarterbacks and was very nervous.

We decided to give Unitas a try-out, along with a large group of other candidates. It took a 75-cent telephone call to contact John, and we wound up with a quarterback who became one of the best in the business.

When I had taken over as head coach of the Colts in 1954, the team had been one of the worst in the NFL. Many changes and adjustments had to be made. I took two defensive ends and made offensive guards out of them.

Then, Gino Marchetti, who was an offensive tackle, was shifted to defensive end. It didn't take long for him to master that position as he became perhaps the greatest defensive end there ever was.

We kept experimenting with our new personnel, and it took time before all the pieces began to fall into the right places.

The team took shape during my fourth year with the Colts, and then, in 1958, we really looked like a team that might go all the way.

At the start of the season, I told the squad that this was a year "to know and be known." By that I meant that if they knew their offense and defense and didn't make errors, they would win games and become known.

And so this squad of cast-offs and never-beens

found itself at Yankee Stadium on December 28, 1958, in the championship play-off game against the glamor team of professional football, an outstanding Giant team.

The Colts had plenty of incentive to win this big one, but a team can always use a little extra stimulus. Charley Conerly, the Giants' quarterback, inadvertently helped us by writing in his regular weekly newspaper column that New York had out-gutted us in winning an earlier season game, 24-21.

There is nothing a ball player resents more than to be accused of lacking guts, and a blow-up of this article on the locker room wall didn't hurt the morale of our team one bit.

Just before they took the field, I reminded our players that they were still considered a bunch of rejects in many circles, and it was up to them to prove otherwise to New York and the entire football world.

We had a chance to get out in front early in the game as a result of a long pass from Unitas to Lenny Moore, but after we gained only five yards on the next three plays, Steve Myrha missed a 27-yard field goal.

Late in that period, Conerly got the Giants' attack moving, but as soon as they were deep in our territory, our defense stiffened. From 36 yards out, Pat Summerall kicked a field goal, giving New York a 3-0 lead, with just a shade over two minutes left in the first quarter.

I felt encouraged about our offense even though

we had not been able to score in the first period. It was apparent that our ball carriers could run between their tackles, and our offensive line was giving Unitas ample time to throw.

We also noticed that after Unitas' first long pass to Moore, the Giants decided to double-team him, leaving Raymond Berry in a more favorable position as a target.

Frank Gifford's fumble on the Giants' 20 gave us a big chance, and six straight running plays brought us our first score, in the second period. Alan Ameche went over from the two, and we led, 7-3, after Myrha's extra point.

The Giants put on another drive, but our tough defense forced Gifford to fumble again. From our own 14, Unitas started a drive which did not stop until he hit Berry for a 15-yard touchdown. Myrha booted the extra point, and we led, 14-3.

It was a good feeling taking that 11-point edge into the dressing room at half-time, but we were not going to be content with protecting that lead in the second half. Our plan was to try to break the game wide open in the third period.

Behind some great blocking. Unitas picked apart the Giant secondary with a wide variety of pass patterns, and we moved to the Giants' three-yard line where it was first and goal to go.

Unitas sent Ameche into the line three times, but those three tries moved us only two yards. Then, on fourth and one, Unitas saw the Giant defense playing in tight and decided to send Ameche out wide on a toss-out. The Giant defense smelled it and reacted well. Their great defensive play, coupled with the partially frozen ground causing poor footing at that end of the field, helped throw Ameche for a four-yard loss. Instead of breaking the game wide open, we turned the ball over to the Giants, who after that tremendous goal-line stand, now had a psychological edge.

Some might have questioned the wisdom of going for the touchdown, instead of a sure field goal which would have given us a 17-3 lead. Well, I was confident that we could get in there and really break the game wide open. Maybe I was just a young coach who was trying to cram it down their throats. Perhaps today, knowing percentages a little better, I might on fourth down go for the three points. Your "hindsight" is always 20-20.

In any event, that goal-line stand gave the Giants a lift. On third and two from his own 13-yard line, Conerly, a great passer, sent Kyle Rote, usually a short receiver, far down field and hit him around mid-field. Rote raced down to the 25 where he ran into a two-man tackle and fumbled the ball. The ball bounded away from all three players, and Giant halfback Alex Webster picked it up and carried it to our one-yard line. The entire play covered a total of 86 yards, and after Mel Triplett plunged over for the touchdown, Summerall kicked the extra point, cutting our lead to 14-10.

I was concerned but not because of the long pass from Conerly to Rote. You've got to expect plays

27

like that to click when you have an outstanding passer and some first-rate receivers.

What worried me more than anything else was the possibility that the Giants' goal-line stand, combined with this quick touchdown, would fire them up and force us to lose our momentum. And every coach knows that once a team loses momentum, regaining it becomes extremely difficult.

My concern was justified. Our smooth offense bogged down. Our near-perfect pass protection for Unitas collapsed. We could do nothing right while the Giants could do nothing wrong.

Conerly called his plays beautifully, hitting end Bob Schnelker for 17 and 46 yards on successive plays to give the Giants a first down on our 15. Then, he passed to Gifford down the sideline for the touchdown. Summerall again added the extra point, and early in the fourth period, the Giants had regained the lead, 17-14.

Our pass protection for Unitas was not much better during most of the final period, and the clock was moving too fast. With less than three minutes left in the game, the Giants had a third down with about four yards to go on their own 40. Gifford was called on to make the big first down which might enable the Giants to run out the clock. Frank swept to his right, and Gino Marchetti got a hand on him to slow him down. Gene (Big Daddy) Lipscomb crashed in to stop Gifford, and when they brought the chains in for the measurement, the Giants were inches short.

Faced with a fourth down and inches to go from their own 43, I am sure that Giants' coach, Jim Lee Howell, did not give any thought to going for the first down. It was too much of a gamble. If they failed, we could quickly be in field-goal range.

On the other hand, the Giants had one of the best punters in the league in Don Chandler, and with time running out, a kick was the only play.

Chandler got off a good one which was downed on our own 14-yard line, and we were 86 long yards away from their goal line with only 1:56 left to play.

I didn't have to give the players any pep talk before their final chance. They knew that this was their big opportunity to prove that they were pretty good rejects, and of course, this was the ideal spot to show that they had plenty of guts. Our attitude was that we were not going to blow this game. All I did was tell Unitas to use our two-minutes-to-go offense.

The Giants were expecting Unitas to pass near the sidelines in order to stop the clock after a completion, but John crossed them up. He sent decoys to the sidelines, and fired away at Berry down the middle. Raymond made three great catches, and we reached the Giants' 13 with time left for only one more play. Myrha rushed into the game to try for the tying field goal from the 20, and there were only seven seconds left when the ball passed through the uprights to send the game into a sudden-death overtime.

29

I had no special instructions for the team before the start of the overtime. I felt that they had regained their momentum and knew the work that had to be done.

The Giants won the toss of the coin but our defense was great, forcing them to give up the ball after three plays failed to get them a first down.

I reminded Unitas that time was no longer a factor and that he could set his own pace.

L.G. Dupre went over right tackle for a first down on the 31. Unitas missed on a long pass to Moore, and Dupre picked up only two to make it third and eight on the 33. Unitas passed to Ameche in the flat, and Alan powered his way to the 41, barely making the first down.

Dupre gained three, but Unitas lost eight trying to pass, and we were pushed back to the 36, faced with a crucial third and 15 situation.

Unitas called for a pass down the right side to Moore, but when he saw Lenny was covered, he looked to his left. Just as he was about to be nailed for another loss, John spotted Berry open down the left side and completed a 20-yard pass for a first down on the Giants' 43.

After lining up for the next play, Unitas noticed Giant linebacker Sam Huff was a few yards deeper than usual, anticipating a pass. It looked like an ideal spot for a trap play so John checked his signals with an audible.

Dick Modzelewski charged in fast as Unitas started to fade back, and he was taken out of the play by our left guard, Art Spinney. George Preas, our right tackle, moved out to cut down Huff as Unitas handed off to Ameche. Alan went 23 yards down the middle to the Giants' 20 on as perfect a call as you will ever see.

Dupre was held without any gain, but Unitas hit Berry on a slant pattern for 10 yards and a first down on the 10.

Time was called, and Unitas came over to the sidelines to ask me what I wanted to do. I guess it was just a courtesy call since I had great faith in John's ability to select the right plays. I simply advised him to keep the ball on the ground and to call safe plays so that we would not be risking a fumble at this stage. If we did not get a touchdown in three plays, it wasn't important. We would settle for an easy field goal.

Unitas went back to the huddle and called a fullback slant which was a safe enough play. Ameche gained only a yard, but that didn't concern me. Two more similar plays, and we could go for our field goal.

Then John dropped back to pass. It's a wonder that I didn't have heart failure as John faded back. What was he up to? A pass was exactly the one thing I didn't want. Three points were just as good as six for us, and not only were we risking an interception but I had visions of our pass protection breaking down, allowing one of the Giants' big linemen to crash through and knock the ball out of Unitas' hand.

However, John lofted the ball to the right flat

31

over two defenders and into the waiting hands of Jim Mutscheller on the one-yard line. That play took only a few seconds, but to me it seemed forever.

Later John explained that the Giants were lined up tight, expecting another running play and that he felt he could catch them off-balance with a pass. He said that he would have thrown the ball out of bounds if he had seen any danger of an interception.

I'm sure that most of the fans who had seen John and me in a huddle before that play assumed that I was responsible for the call. If it had boomeranged, I know that John would have accepted full blame, so I guess I'll have to give him all the credit, too.

From the one-yard line, it was easy for Ameche. Unitas called for our 16 power play which was designed for use against tight goal-line defenses, and with Moore leading some perfect blocking, Ameche went between his right tackle and end to score standing up.

Nobody even bothered about the extra point, and at eight minutes and 15 seconds of the overtime, the Baltimore Colts had won their first NFL championship.

For 11 years, that game remained unchallenged as my most memorable one. Then, along came the Super Bowl in Miami on January 12th, 1969, and although I was tempted to name it as my No. 1 choice, it was just impossible to select one of these great games over the other.

Beating the Colts in the Super Bowl was truly a storybook thing for me. It was only natural for me to receive great personal satisfaction in knocking off a ball club whose owner had suddenly fired me after I had developed it into a championship team.

It also meant a great deal to all of us in becoming the first American Football League team to win the Super Bowl. Before this game, quite a few football fans, coaches, players and writers felt the NFL was far superior to the AFL and really believed that it would be years before an AFL representative would have a chance in the Super Bowl.

Many self-designated experts were saying that the Jets did not belong on the same field with the Colts, who, after setting a league record by winning 15 games that season, were being rated on a par with Vince Lombardi's most powerful Green Bay teams.

Some writers recalling the failures of Kansas City and Oakland in the first two Super Bowls, went so far as to call this the worst mis-match possible for the world's championship.

None of these stories bothered me. In fact, I liked them. Most coaches prefer the role of the underdog. When you are made the overwhelming favorite, you always are in a position where the players become complacent and will let down.

We had no such problem even though Pete Lammons, our tight end, told me to stop showing the movies of the Colts' games so often or else our team would get overconfident.

That was our attitude. It was apparent that Baltimore was a fine football team, but from watching their films, we felt certain that they were not as invincible as claimed by the newspapermen.

There was much comment about Joe Namath's pre-game statement in which he not only said that we would win the game but he would guarantee it.

I wished at that time he had not said it publicly because I wanted the Baltimore players to feel that they were the greatest. If they became too cocky, it would be easier for us to chop them down to size.

But Joe's an honest kid, and when he's asked a question, he gives an honest answer. He doesn't say anything that he doesn't mean.

Along with the rest of the squad and the coaches, Joe spent hours studying the Baltimore films, trying to pick up flaws in their awesome defense.

Part of our game plan called for the concentration of our running attack to the left. We reached this decision in part because of the Baltimore personnel but mainly because our best strength was to that side.

No new plays were designed for our passing game. We were certain that Joe could throw against Baltimore, and although we wanted the Colts to think that we had some new wrinkles in store for them, we were ready to go with the basic patterns used during the regular season.

As in all my game plans, I try to get balance between our running and passing game, but it doesn't always work out this way. Sometimes the score or the time-to-go dictates otherwise.

In any event, Namath is pretty much on his own during a game. He is as smart a quarterback as there is in the business, and once he is given the game plan, he can be depended upon to carry it out.

His signal calling could not have been better against the Colts. He kept coming back to the plays which had been working well, and he kept making the big play all afternoon.

During the week before the Super Bowl, I kept reminding the players that poise and execution would win for them. I emphasized that they must never lose their poise even if Baltimore should get a couple of quick scores. And it was equally important that they not get angry if the officials should rule against us on a key play. No matter how adverse the situation might be, victory could still be ours if we remained cool.

The squad was told time and again that flawless execution of our plays was necessary in order to score. I warned the players not to go into the game depending upon the opponents to make mistakes. It was up to us to force Baltimore to commit errors, and this could best be accomplished by proper execution of our game plan.

We had some uneasy moments the first time Baltimore got the ball. Earl Morrall screen passed to tight end John Mackey for 19 yards; Tom Matte swept for 10; Jerry Hill picked up 10; Morrall hit Jimmy Orr for 15, and very quickly, the Colts had a first down on our 19.

The writers in the press box who had been panning us all week must have felt very smug at this point. The Colts looked like a powerhouse, determined to live up to all their advance notices.

However, our defense suddenly tightened and held on the next three plays. Lou Michaels tried a 27-yard field goal, but it was off line. We had passed our first test.

Baltimore had another big chance late in the first period when George Sauer fumbled on our 12 after catching a sideline pass. Two plays gained only four yards, and on third and six, Morrall tried to hit Tom Mitchell in the end zone. Al Atkinson, our fine middlebacker, deflected the thrown ball and it bounced off Mitchell's shoulder. Randy Beverly picked it off for a touchback.

We had stopped the Colts again. Now, it was time for Joe to get us moving. He called on Matt Snell four times in a row, and Matt powered his way over our left side each time, moving the ball from our 20 to our 46. Our game plan was beginning to take shape.

Joe mixed his plays beautifully. On third and four from Baltimore's 48, he passed to Sauer for 14 and a first down on their 34. Baltimore double-teamed Don Maynard so Joe went to Sauer again, this time for 11 yards. After Emerson Boozer gained two yards, Joe passed to Snell for 12 yards and a first down on the nine. Snell rushed for five and then swept the left side from the four for the first score of the day. Jim Turner added the extra point.

There were still nine minutes left in the first half, and when Tom Matte got through the line of scrimmage and went 58 yards down the sidelines to the 16, our lead didn't look too comfortable.

However, once again our great defense came through for us, and on first down, Johnny Sample intercepted Morrall's pass.

The Colts were still battling to get on the scoreboard as time was running out. With less than a minute left in the half, they tried a bit of razzle-dazzle on what they called the flea-flicker play.

Despite our success in stopping this play all week in practice, Morrall and Matte flipped the ball back and forth as Orr raced downfield. Due to a missed coverage, he broke into the clear at the goal line just as our lineman was catching up with Morrall. Earl apparently could not spot Orr and passed, instead, to his secondary receiver, Jerry Hill, who appeared open. However, Jim Hudson wasn't fooled and picked off the third interception of the period against Morrall.

I was satisfied with the way the team had played during the first half, but I was afraid that seven points would not be enough. We had to be the aggressor and keep the pressure on Baltimore all the way.

We had been able to run and pass well during the first half, and I felt no need to change our game plan for the final 30 minutes. Baltimore's vaunted blitzes had been negated by Joe's quick wrists and the favorable reactions of our receivers. Furthermore, if the Colts continued to double-team Maynard, Joe could go to other targets as he did so successfully in the first two periods.

I was proud of our defense. If they could just

match their first-half performance, Baltimore would not be able to beat us.

On the first play from scrimmage in the third period, our defense gave every indication that it would be just as rough on Baltimore as it was in the first half. Matte, who had scared us with a 58-yard run in the second quarter, was hit hard, fumbling to us on his 33.

We moved to the 25 but were forced to settle for Turner's 32-yard field goal. Then, near the end of the period, Jim booted one from the 30 to give us a 13-0 lead.

It was hardly a safe margin, and I hoped that Namath could get us on the board again. I don't think anyone can call Joe a conservative quarterback, but in the final period, he certainly wasn't taking any chances. He stuck with the running plays which had been working the first three periods and moved us down to the Colts' 2.

A touchdown at this stage would just about ice it for us, but Baltimore held, and Turner kicked his third field goal.

It was now 16-0, but with almost 11 minutes left to play, you know from past experience that you still can't relax.

In the hopes of getting the team moving, Baltimore called on John Unitas, whose sore elbow had kept him sidelined most of the season, but John's first series ended in disaster as Randy Beverly made his second interception of the game.

Sticking to his ground game, Namath used up four

and one-half minutes before turning the ball over to Unitas. The Colts then drove 80 yards, but it took 14 plays, and when Hill scored from the one, three minutes and 19 seconds remained on the clock.

Nine points seemed like a safe enough margin until Lou Michaels' on-side kick was recovered by the Colts on our 44. With Unitas—even an ailing Unitas—anything could happen.

John hit Richardson, Orr, and Richardson again, and Baltimore had a first down on our 19. Then our defense went to work. Sample knocked away a pass intended for Richardson. Strong rushes forced Unitas to throw short and then too long. On a fourth down pass intended for Orr in the end zone, Larry Grantham leaped high to bat the ball down.

With two minutes left to play, Namath used Snell on six straight running plays, and only 15 seconds were left when we were forced to punt. Two plays later it was all history.

A great team effort had proven to the football world what we knew for some time: The New York Jets were No. 1.

George Wilson

1960 NFL Game
Detroit 20, Baltimore 15

George Wilson spent more than 30 years in professional football as a player and coach.

After starring at end for Northwestern University, he played 10 seasons with the Chicago Bears. From 1937 through 1946, he caught 111 passes for 15 touchdowns and was considered one of the best blockers in the game.

In 1947 and 1948, he was an assistant coach at Chicago under George Halas, and in 1949, he moved over to Detroit where he was an assistant until 1957 when he took over the head coaching spot.

The Lions won the National Football League championship during Wilson's first season as head coach, and he was named "Coach of the Year" in the NFL.

His Lions were runners-up in the Western Division from 1960 through 1962, and in each of those three years, they won the Playoff Bowl in Miami.

Wilson's eight-year record as head of the Lions included 57 victories, 45 defeats and six ties.

He spent the 1965 season as an assistant coach with the Washington Redskins, and in 1966, he was named the first head coach of the Miami Dolphins.

The Dolphins won 12 games during Wilson's first three seasons, which was regarded as an outstanding record for an expansion team.

Since leaving football in 1970, Wilson has been engaged in business in Miami.

Detroit won the National Football League championship in 1957, making my first year as a head coach a most memorable one, but Detroit's almost unbelievable last-second victory over Baltimore on December 4, 1960, must stand out as the single biggest and most exciting contest of my coaching career.

This had been a "must" game for us. With a 4-5 record, we trailed Baltimore by two games and needed this win in order to keep our title hopes alive.

It was a crucial game for the Colts, too. They were leading our Western Division with a 6-3 record, just one game in front of Green Bay and San Francisco, and could not afford another loss.

Furthermore, Coach Weeb Ewbank and the Colts

had their sights set on becoming the first team in NFL history to win three consecutive league championships.

I knew what this meant to Weeb and the Colts. I had been in a similar position both as a player and a coach. I played under George Halas for the Chicago Bears when we won the title in 1940 and 1941 but failed in 1942, and I was an assistant coach at Detroit during their championship years of 1952 and 1953 only to miss out in 1954.

While all regular season games are important, there are always a few which take on special significance. Baltimore, with a reputation as an established top contender and with a great quarterback named Johnny Unitas, always heightened our desire to win.

Although we had beaten the Colts earlier in the season, we expected a rough afternoon in Baltimore and spent the week prior to the game working as though it were for a championship event.

You know you are going to have your hands full any time you play against Unitas. I had coached him in the 1958 Pro Bowl game in Los Angeles and learned that in addition to being one of the top quarterbacks ever to enter the ranks of professional football, he had the great ability of getting the rest of the squad up for a ball game.

We spent much of that week with our defensive players, knowing that if they came through with the type of game they were capable of playing, we could beat the Colts and stay in the running for the title.

I was proud of our defensive unit and felt it was one of the best in the game. These players had been together for about five years and from this experience learned each other's moves. They reacted automatically in almost any given situation.

The captain and the great leader of our defensive team was Joe Schmidt, who is now Detroit's head coach. He was most adept in reading offenses and shifting our defensive alignment accordingly, but perhaps his greatest asset was his team pride, which he, in turn, instilled in his unit.

This is the starting defensive team we used against the Colts:

Left End—Darris McCord
Left Tackle—Roger Brown
Right Tackle—Alex Karras
Right End—Bill Glass
Left Linebacker—Carl Brettschneider
Middle Linebacker—Joe Schmidt
Right Linebacker—Wayne Walker
Left Cornerback—Night Train Lane
Strong Safety—Gary Lowe
Weak Safety—Yale Lary
Right Cornerback—Ricky LeBeau

If our offense could get us a few points, I was confident that the defense would hold the Colts in check.

I always worry about my players the night before a game. There was an additional problem in Baltimore, where many parties were being held in the same hotel where we were staying. All the noise and festivity was a major concern, since all athletes need a good night's sleep in order to be alert and at their best the next day.

I also was worried because I found it difficult deciding between Jim Ninowski and Earl Morrall as our starting quarterback.

Jim had a much stronger arm and was a better runner than Earl. However, Earl, in his fourth year as a pro, was a dedicated student of the game. He spent a great deal of time examining game films on his own after the rest of the squad had viewed them. Earl always made a careful study of the personnel he would be facing and could predict the type of defenses that a team would be using against us. He mixed his plays very well and would always call a good game.

I liked Morrall because of his tremendous spirit. Even though he did not start a game and might not see any action until late in the third or fourth quarter, I don't know of any other second-string quarterback who had his ability to ignite a team late in a game.

After carefully considering the daily performances of both Ninowski and Morrall during the past week's practice sessions, I decided to start Ninowski and keep Morrall in reserve, ready to go in if the team needed a lift.

The next morning at the pre-game meal I was relieved to find that the players had managed to get their needed sleep despite the clamor which had echoed through the hotel corridors until the wee hours of the morning.

On the bus ride to the stadium and while the players were dressing for the game, hardly anyone uttered a sound. It was the type of tension that I have always found prevalent before a big game. I like to see my players keyed up like this since they seem to come through with an extra effort under these conditions.

I didn't feel it necessary to do more than review our game plan before we took the field.

As anticipated, the game quickly became a defensive struggle. Early in the first period, Yale Lary, our excellent punter, dropped back to kick from our own goal line on a fourth and 16 situation, but Lebron Shield, whom we had released before the start of the season, eluded our blockers and came through so fast that Lary never had a chance. Shield blocked the kick, and the ball rolled out of the end zone for an automatic safety, giving the Colts a 2-0 lead.

We fought back in the same period, starting a drive on our own 20-yard line and moving all the way to the Baltimore 12 before the Colts' defense tightened up. Forced to go for the field goal, Jim Martin obliged from the 20-yard line, putting us in front by what looked more like a hockey score, 3-2.

The second period wasn't very old when the Colts erased that lead. Unitas, passing from his own 20, hit Lenny Moore in the flat, and Moore, helped by some key blocks by Jerry Richardson and Gary

Lowe, raced 80 yards down the right sideline for the touchdown. Dick (Night Train) Lane blocked the Myrha's attempt for the extra point, and Baltimore led, 8-3.

The Colts had two other chances in that first period, but our strong defense held them on our 18 and 24.

We then started to move the ball and went all the way to the Colts' seven-yard line where we had four downs to get a score. On the first play, Ninowski dropped back to pass and was nailed for a seven-yard loss. Then, he tried to pass again, and this time, Bobby Boyd intercepted and returned the ball 74 yards to our 12-yard line.

As so frequently happens in football, the team that had been threatening to score suddenly finds itself backed against the wall a minute later.

But the tide reversed itself once again, as Unitas fumbled on the first play and Roger Brown recovered for us.

The half ended with Baltimore leading, 8-3, and that's the way it remained until the fourth quarter.

In that final period, we received a second opportunity when Lebeau intercepted a Unitas pass and ran it back to the Colts' 40. At that point, I decided to send Morrall in as quarterback to see if he could get our offense moving. Dependable Earl did just that. He sent flanker back Howard (Hopalong) Cassady down deep, and when Cassady got behind Milt Davis and Johnny Sample, Morrall hit him with a perfect 40-yard pass for our first touchdown. Martin's extra

46

point put us ahead by two points, 10-8.

Then, it was back to a defensive struggle, and neither team could do much until late in the period when Martin booted a 47-yard field goal for us with 1:18 left to play. It looked like that was the ball game since it meant the Colts could no longer beat us with a field goal but would have to go all the way for a touchdown.

We kicked off confident that victory was ours, and Baltimore took over on its own 20-yard line—80 long yards away from our goal line. It must have looked even further away for the Colts after Unitas missed twice in trying to hit Moore with passes, and there was only a minute left in the game.

But on third and 10, Unitas kept the Colts' chance alive with a 19-yard pass to Jim Mutscheller. We helped them along with a holding violation, and after a Unitas to Moore pass just missed by inches, Unitas faked to Moore and passed to Ray Berry, who stepped out-of-bounds on our 45 to stop the clock.

The same play gained seven yards to our 38, and again stopped the clock with only 29 seconds to play. On the next play, Lebeau did a fine job of defending against Berry, and Unitas over-shot him. There were only 22 seconds left, and that 47-yard field goal kept looking bigger all the time.

But you always have to be worried when you're up against a quarterback like Unitas. He dropped back and lofted a lead pass to Moore, who was racing towards our goal line. Night Train Lane stayed with him step for step. As Lenny hit the goal line, he was actually outstretched in mid-air as he dove about six feet towards the ball. Lane, a great defensive back, dove right along with Moore, but was inches behind, and those few inches made the difference.

Moore made one of the most spectacular catches that I have ever seen, and what had seemed like a certain victory for us now loomed as a certain defeat. Myrha kicked the extra point to make it, 15-13, as the fans poured out of the stands and out onto the playing field.

The security forces cleared the field, but the crowd was still milling at least 20 deep along the sidelines.

There were just 14 seconds left when Myrha kicked off to our one, and we ran it back 34 yards to our 35.

With all times-out used, Morrall knew that this had to be a "do or die" play for us. He sent Gail Cogdill, our spread end and one of the fastest men on our squad, out to the right side, put Terry Barr to the left as a flanker and Jim Gibbons at the strongside left end.

Gibbons at that time was probably one of the best strongside ends in the game. He was not the type of player who had great speed like Cogdill, but his sure hands and good moves made up for any lack of speed.

There was no reason for anyone to expect anything but a long, desperation pass to Cogdill.

We were 65 yards away from the Baltimore goal line

with only 14 seconds left, and the Colts were expecting just such a play and lined up against us with a four-man front line, two outside linebackers and five deep secondary men.

Cogdill ran directly across the field and far down the left side, taking Baltimore's defensive secondary along with him. That left Gibbons wide open as he crossed over to the right side.

Nobody was close to Gibbons when he caught the ball on the Baltimore 35, and time had expired as he easily made it into the end zone all by himself. Martin went through the formality of kicking the extra point to give us this great 20-15 victory.

Of course, Morrall had taken a terrific gamble, calling for the shorter pass in a situation where we would never have had enough time to get off another play if Gibbons had not gone all the way. It took plenty of courage for Morrall to call the play, but it wound up catching everybody off guard.

On the next page is a diagram of that game-winning play.

This was one of the greatest calls a quarterback could have made in such a situation. Earl not only fooled everybody in the stands, but more important, everybody on Baltimore's defensive unit. When Morrall was asked later why he called this play instead of going for the bomb, he simply replied that he thought it would work.

Although this was one of our most exciting finishes, ironically enough I didn't even get to see the last play until we looked at the movies the next day.

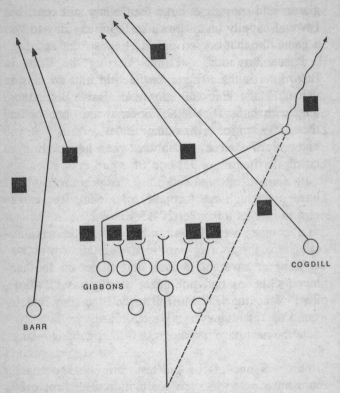

COGDILL

GIBBONS

BARR

With the increased numbers on the sidelines, I had found myself, along with several members of the team, in the rear of a human wall of fans. Being as anxious as the spectators to see what was happening, I managed to do my share of pushing as I was frantically struggling to get through the mob.

When I finally did emerge, I was completely dishevelled and found myself minus my tie clasp and glasses and sporting a large tear in my suit coat, but I would happily take losses like those any day to win a game like that one.

It was an additional thrill beating the Colts in Baltimore; much akin to the feeling a team gets in defeating the Packers in Green Bay. Both these teams have fanatically loyal fans who are behind them 100 per cent, and they make certain that you know from start to finish that you are playing in enemy territory.

In the locker room following the game, you would have thought that we had just won the league championship. The players were every bit as jubilant as they were in 1957 when they had beaten Cleveland for the title.

The victory against Baltimore gave us the momentum to go on and defeat the Dallas Cowboys, 23-14, and the Chicago Bears, 36-0, in our remaining regular season games; and then in the first Runner-Up Bowl in Miami, we edged Cleveland, 17-16.

Baltimore never did recover from its last second loss to us and dropped its next two games, missing its chance to be the first team in pro history to win three championships in a row.

Sports writers called this Baltimore-Detroit game "fantastic," "unbelievable," "incredible," and used many other similar adjectives.

Personally, I feel privileged to have been a part of a game which has gone down in pro football history as one of the most exciting finishes of all time.

Norm Van Brocklin

1961 NFL Game
Minnesota 37, Chicago 13

Norm Van Brocklin has been part of the National Football League scene since 1949 when he was the fourth draft choice of the Los Angeles Rams.

Although an All-America quarterback at the University of Oregon, he was by-passed during the early rounds of the draft, and later he made many teams regret this mistake.

Van Brocklin became one of the greats in the game, and in 1969 was rated along with Sammy Baugh as runner-up to Johnny Unitas as pro football's all-time quarterback.

At Los Angeles, Van Brocklin shared the quarterback spot with Bob Waterfield in 1949, 1950 and 1951 as the Rams won the Western Division titles. It was Van Brocklin's 73-yard touchdown pass to Tom Fears in the final period that gave the Rams a 24–17 win over Cleveland in the playoff for the NFL championship in 1951.

Three years after being traded to Philadel-

NORM VAN BROCKLIN

phia, his 35-yard touchdown pass to Tommy
McDonald lifted the Eagles to a 17—13 victory over Green Bay for the 1960 NFL crown.

He retired as a player after that game and
became the first head coach of the expansion
Minnesota Vikings. After six seasons with the
Vikings, he resigned, stayed out of coaching
for a year, and then came to Atlanta during
the 1968 season. In 1969, during his first
full season with the Falcons, he guided the
team to a 6—8 record, including a win over
Minnesota, the NFL champions.

Van Brocklin was born March 15, 1926,
in Parade, S.D.

Some coaches must wait many years before they
participate in a game which they will always want to
remember. I didn't have to wait very long for my
most memorable game as a coach. It was my very
first one.

There are a number of reasons why I will never
forget this game at Bloomington, Minnesota, on
September 17th, 1961, when the Minnesota Vikings
upset the Chicago Bears, 37-13.

Not only was this my debut in the National Football League as a coach but it was the first official
game for the newly formed Viking team, a squad of
cast-offs and rookies competing as an expansion club

53

against one of the best organizations in pro football.

It was a tremendous challenge for a young coach like myself to oppose George Halas, one of the greatest football coaches of all time. In fact, it was a wonderful feeling just having the chance to be pitted against a coach who is regarded as the George Washington of professional football.

That victory over George Halas and the Chicago Bears in our very first league game gave our entire ball club a big lift. It provided the recognition we needed to get started in a state where the fans had long been accustomed to the finest in football tradition as exemplified by the University of Minnesota.

Everybody was looking at us from an expansion stand-point. Many thought that we would be fortunate to win a single game all season since our squad was composed mainly of players unwanted by the other teams in the NFL.

Many of the personnel came to Minnesota with the reputation of being malcontents. Some were regarded as misfits.

It was far from an encouraging situation for a freshman coach who, as a player, had been associated with championship teams at Los Angeles and Philadelphia.

I was somewhat apprehensive when our squad assembled for pre-season practice. Some players had experience in pro ball; others didn't. I had no experience as a coach, but I knew that one of my primary jobs would be to communicate with the players and to motivate them.

The squad soon became well aware of my philosophy of coaching. First and foremost, I made them realize that our success and future depended upon hard work and self-discipline. Unless a player was willing to give 100 per cent every minute, there would be no reward. If he did not have enough self-discipline or if I were unable to discipline him, he would be a liability to the team and would not be around very long.

I tried to create a togetherness feeling among the players. I knew the importance of a strong esprit de corps from my experience as a player the year before at Philadelphia. We won the NFL title that year when we weren't that good a football club. But what we did possess was tremendous team spirit. Everybody was for each other, and this more than any other factor carried us to the championship.

I hoped that the same esprit de corps would develop among the players at Minnesota.

The five pre-season exhibition games would be used as a period of experimentation. I told the players that I did not care if we lost them all. They did not count.

In that short period, we had to mold our offensive and defensive players into smooth units which would be ready to face 14 veteran NFL teams during the regular season.

We dropped all five exhibition games, but we learned a great deal from these defeats, especially from our 30-7 loss to the Bears just two weeks prior to our league opener against them.

That game was close enough to the season opener for the Bears to have most of their defenses set, and we were able to document the style of play we could expect from them.

We spent every minute available studying the film of our game against the Bears and film of other Chicago games, and we found that the Bears not only liked to blitz but would use six- and seven-man blitzes. Sometimes they even threw their safety man in there.

Our game plan was based strictly on the recognition of Chicago's blitzes. We decided to concentrate our offense against their weak side, picking up their free safety with our spread end. We would hit them frequently with screen passes.

As it turned out, we hurt them with our audibles. I guess they thought that they could intimidate us and kept coming after us with their blitzes, but we were ready for them.

The powerful Chicago offense presented some serious problems in our attempt to set up effective defenses. As an expansion club, we did not have as many top players as our opponent. Our secondary was especially weak. Against passes, we would cover their receivers, man for man, with a little double teaming from time to time. Occasionally, we would blitz.

Our defensive front line would have to exert constant pressure, outhit the Bears and cause them to make mistakes.

If we could play defense, we would have a chance

to win. If we did not play defense, we did not stand a chance.

In the dressing room before our first official game, there was some tenseness among the players, as might be expected from an expansion club. We reviewed our game plan before taking the field. There was no pep talk. We had spent the week trying to get the players up for the game, and if they weren't ready by game time, it was too late for any words of inspiration.

We shocked the Bears by scoring early in the first period, and we never allowed them to recover. We had to settle for Mike Mercer's 12-yard field goal after stalling on the Bears' five-yard line, but we were on the scoreboard first.

We had another scoring chance after the ensuing kickoff when a bad snap from Chicago's center sailed over the punter's head for a 33-yard loss. We took over on the 19, but George Shaw was unable to move the team, and we had to go for the field goal once again. This time Mercer's kick from the 19 failed.

In just a few plays, we had another scoring opportunity when Clancy Osborne intercepted a pass on the Chicago 20-yard line. At this point I decided to make a change at quarterback. Shaw had been able to get us only three points, and I knew that we needed much more against a Chicago offense which could explode any minute. I called on Fran Tarkenton, a rookie who was very ambitious and hungry at that time.

Tarkenton moved the ball well on his first series, and we quickly found ourselves facing a fourth and goal situation from the Bears' one.

I play primarily percentage football, and most of the time I would go for a field goal, but in this situation with an expansion club, we needed as many points as we could get in a hurry. We had the momentum, and I thought that a touchdown might bust the game wide open.

I did not think that we were taking too much of a risk by trying for the touchdown instead of the field goal. If a run failed, the Bears would be in a big hole. It would then give our defense a chance to hold them and possibly force them to fumble or throw the ball away.

Tarkenton tried to take the ball over himself, but the Bears were waiting for him, and he failed to make it.

The first quarter ended with Minnesota clinging to its 3-0 lead, but early in the second period, we had our first touchdown.

Tarkenton, in carrying out our game plan of calling audibles against the Chicago blitzes, moved the ball to the Bears' 10-yard line, from where he hit Bob Snelker with a perfect pass in the end zone. Mercer added the extra point, and at 1:27 of the second quarter, we were in front, 10-0.

The Bears came roaring back, driving 66 yards in 13 plays. Rick Casares scored from the three, and although the extra point was missed, our 10-6 lead was far from being comfortable.

However, our defense tightened up. We played the Bears on even terms the rest of the period and took the 10-6 lead into the dressing room at half-time.

We didn't make any change in our game plan during the intermission. We were satisfied with the way things were working for us. The half-time was more of a reassuring period for us. Some of the older fellows we had picked up from other teams had been skeptical about our game plan. That was to be expected. But when they saw the results in the first half, it gave them confidence and made them feel that we were probably on the right track.

If we could go out and execute in the final half as well as we had in the first half, we could win.

I had no intention of playing a conservative, ball control type of game, trying to protect our lead. We needed more points, and we had to go after them.

I certainly didn't have to worry about my players' becoming over-confident and letting down in the second half. That's one problem you never face with an expansion club. The rookies battle all the way, and the rejects try their best to show that the team which dropped them had made a mistake.

The Bears received the second half kickoff, but on the first play from scrimmage, Rip Hawkins nailed Willie Galimore with a fierce tackle, forcing him to fumble, and Rich Mostardi recovered for us on the Chicago 27.

We lost two yards on two running plays, and on third and 12 from the 29, Tarkenton lofted a pass to Jerry Reichow, who out-raced J. C. Caroline and

Rick Pettibone to make the catch in the corner of the end zone.

I'm sure that the Bears had come out for the second half determined to show the upstart expansion club a thing or two, but our ability to capitalize so quickly on their fumble cooled them off.

There was still plenty of time left in the game, but I felt that we were in control.

Late in the period, we added another touchdown on some fine passing by Tarkenton. A Chicago blitz almost nailed him for a big loss, but he broke away from several linemen to throw a 49-yard pass to Reichow on the Bears' two-yard line.

Three plays failed to move the ball. Faced with a fourth and two situation, Tarkenton rolled out, with the option of running or passing. He spotted McElhenny open in the end zone, hit him with a perfect strike, and we led, 24-6, going into the last quarter.

Charley Summer's pass interception set up our fourth touchdown at the start of the final quarter. On another roll-out, Tarkenton this time decided to run the ball and scored from the two, carrying two Bears with him.

Our final touchdown came on a two-yard pass from Tarkenton to Middleton. Fran faked a running play and then tossed to Middleton, our outside receiver, who was all alone in the end zone.

The Bears managed to score after the next kickoff, but that was it. We wound up winning, 37-13.

It was difficult to believe. The Minnesota Vikings,

a brand new franchise with rookies and cast-offs, had not only upset the powerful Chicago Bears in their very first league game but they had done it decisively.

Rookie quarterback Tarkenton had shown the poise of a veteran in following our game plan and in calling audibles. However, it was far from a one-man victory. Our defense had been superb, never letting up in harassing the Bears.

It was a magnificent team victory and one I will never forget.

Wally Lemm

1961 AFL Championship Game
Houston 10, San Diego 3

With the exception of the 1957 and 1958 seasons, Wally Lemm coached in the pro football ranks from 1956 until the end of the 1970 campaign when he retired.

In 1956 as defensive backfield coach of the Chicago Cardinals, his secondary was rated the best in the National Football League as it set a modern record in allowing just nine touchdowns on passes. It also was first with most interceptions (33).

He served as athletic director and head coach at Lake Forest College in 1957 and '58, rejoining the Cardinals in 1959 in St. Louis.

Lemm moved to Houston as defensive backfield coach in 1960, but he left after just one season to enter private business. He was named head coach of the Oilers after the first five games of the 1961 season, taking a team with a 1–3–1 record and leading it to 10 straight victories and the American Football League title.

He returned to the Cardinals once again,

this time as their head coach, in 1962. The best of four years with St. Louis was 1964 when the Cardinals compiled an 8–3–2 record in finishing as division runners-up. They then defeated Green Bay in the NFL Playoff Bowl.

In 1966, Lemm was back as head coach of the Oilers, and remained with Houston until his retirement.

His record as a head coach in pro ball includes 66 victories, 66 defeats, and seven ties.

A graduate of Carroll College where he was a halfback, Lemm later became head coach at Montana State where he served during 1954 and 1955.

Looking back over ten years as a head coach in both the National and American Football Leagues, there are a number of games that stand out as being memorable.

I had to consider my first win as a head coach over the Dallas Texans (now the Kansas City Chiefs), a couple of wins over the Green Bay Packers in the Vince Lombardi era, some wins over the Cleveland Browns when Jim Brown was in his prime, and a couple of wins over the New York Giants in the days of Y.A. Tittle and company.

A pre-season game win over the Chicago Bears at Soldiers' Field also was strong in my mind as well as a shutout of Joe Namath and the New York Jets in 1966.

One of the most rewarding victories that I, my staff and my team have ever had was a decisive win over the Packers in the Playoff Bowl in Miami in January of 1965 when I was with the St. Louis Cardinals.

Victory in this game was sweet because pro football teams at that time were all measured against the Pack from Green Bay with their great stars—Bart Starr, Jim Taylor, Ray Nitschke, Boyd Dowler, Max McGee and so many others.

The St. Louis Cardinals, a young team under the leadership of quarterback Charley Johnson, were in control all the way through the game and although I won't say we won easily, we won decisively.

I had many times felt that this was the finest win I had had up to this point. However, when I look back with a great deal of concentration, I find that I have to go back to my first year as a head coach in the pros and pick as my most memorable game the championship playoff between the Houston Oilers and San Diego Chargers at the close of the 1961 season.

In all the years that I have worked as an assistant or head coach in professional football, I have to rate this game as the most vicious, hard-hitting football game I have ever seen. A total of 13 players were injured during the game. At one time, Houston had seven men sidelined with injuries.

And as a further indication of the tremendous defensive play on the part of both teams, there were ten pass interceptions—six of them against George Blanda—and a total of seven fumbles in the game.

I don't mean to infer that this was the best game I have witnessed nor that the 1961 Oilers and Chargers were the greatest teams that have ever stepped on a field, but I believe that the game itself was played with more ferocity than I had ever seen before or since.

Houston had some very fine players, led by George Blanda at quarterback, who by the way is probably the fiercest competitor it has ever been my pleasure to coach.

We also had fine competitors and performers in Charley Tolar, Billy Cannon, Charley Hennigan, Bill Groman, Don Floyd, Ed Husmann, Dennis Morris, Bob Talamini and Hogan Wharton, to mention only a few.

San Diego, at this time, was quarterbacked by Jack Kemp and they also had their share of hard-nosed, first-class competitors. The game became more violent as it progressed and the hitting could literally be heard in the stands.

It was early in the history of the American Football League and the so-called experts of the game were laughing up their collective sleeves at the up-start league and were being hypercritical of the defensive players.

In this championship game, played on December 24, 1961, I have to state strongly that overall it was one of the best played defensive struggles that I have ever seen.

It marked the second straight year that the Oilers and Chargers had met for the American Football League championship. Houston captured the AFL's first championship in 1960 by beating the Chargers (then the Los Angeles Chargers), 24-16.

The following year, San Diego won the Western Division with a fine 12-2 record. At one point during the season, the Chargers had a 15-game winning streak, including four pre-season triumphs, but the Oilers snapped that streak with a solid 33-13 win before a record crowd of 37,845 in Houston.

While the Chargers encountered little trouble in winning their division title by a six-game margin over second place Dallas (6-8), Houston had been forced down to the wire in the Eastern Division by second-place Boston.

Houston had started poorly, winning only one of its first five games and tying one. Then, I was named head coach, and we won the last nine games in a row to finish with a 10-3-1 record, just one game ahead of the Boston Patriots, who were 9-4-1.

The championship game was played in Balboa Stadium in San Diego, and the pressure was on us not only as the defending champions but because we had not lost a game since I had taken over as coach.

We received a break early in the game when Dalva Allen recovered a fumble by Kemp on the Charger

37, but San Diego regained possession of the ball almost immediately when Bud Whitehead picked off a Blanda pass and ran it back 41 yards to the 49.

Kemp passed to his tight end Dave Kocourek on a delayed screen, and Dave ran 43 yards before we could stop him on the eight-yard line.

Kemp then tried to put San Diego on the scoreboard with a pass to Luther Hayes in the end zone, but Freddy Glick, our defensive halfback, stepped in front of Hayes for a fine interception which ended that threat.

We had a chance to score later in the first period when Doug Cline recovered another fumble by Kemp. We were able to gain only five yards in three plays, and on a fake field goal attempt, the pass from center sailed over Bill Groman's head.

A pass interception stopped us in the second period after we had moved the ball 39 yards to the San Diego 22. Blanda attempted to hit Cannon in the end zone, but Charley McNeil had other ideas and made the interception.

Mid-way in the second quarter, we were given another chance when we rushed Paul Maguire, who was back to punt, and the ball sliced off his foot, going only nine yards to the San Diego 39.

Once again, the Chargers stopped us, but this time Blanda successfully booted a 46-yard field goal to put us in front, 3-0, with 6:44 left in the half.

San Diego had two more opportunities to score before the half ended. On their first try, the Chargers moved to our 36, but Cline stopped that drive with an interception. Then, seconds before the half ended, George Blair attempted a field goal from our 44, but missed, allowing us to take a 3-0 lead into the dressing room.

Early in the third quarter, we stopped San Diego again when Mark Johnston intercepted a Kemp pass on our 22. Then Blanda passed to Groman for eight yards, and San Diego was caught for pass interference, giving us the ball on the Charger 35-yard line. But Whitehead intercepted Blanda's first down pass, and we had to count on our defense to get the ball back for us.

Our great defensive unit did just that, and we started a drive on our own 20. This time we didn't stop until we scored what proved to be the game's only touchdown. However, we had a close call midway during the drive. It was fourth down and inches to go on the San Diego 40, and Charlie Tolar came through to give us the big first down, enabling us to continue all the way.

Cannon picked up five yards on a pitchout. On the next play, Blanda, under tremendous pressure as he was all afternoon, was forced out of his protective pocket and, after rolling out, turned and threw the ball across the field to Cannon, who was a secondary receiver on the play. Billy made a leaping catch of the ball on the San Diego 17, knocked off one tackler, and literally flew into the end zone for what turned out to be the winning score. Blanda added the extra point, giving us a 10-0 lead which we took into the fourth quarter.

We went into that final 15 minutes, fully aware that a great passer like Kemp might get the San Diego offense moving at any time. So instead of playing a conservative game and trying to hold on to our lead, we decided to go after more points.

We were moving the ball well, but McNeil intercepted Blanda's pass on his own 47 and returned it to our 38. Kemp passed to Jim Norton, who made a great catch on the 10-yard line.

Our defenses tightened up at that point, and after San Diego failed to make more than five yards on three plays, Blair came in to kick a field goal, cutting our lead down to 10-3.

There was still plenty of time left. The scoreboard clock showed 14:21 remaining in the fourth period, more than enough time for San Diego to beat us, so we kept trying to get on the scoreboard again.

Once more, we got another good drive moving, but as on five other occasions, Blanda was rushed and had another pass intercepted. This time, it was Bob Zeman who grabbed the ball on the one-yard line to keep us from building up a more comfortable lead.

From this point Kemp mounted a drive which carried the Chargers from their own one to the San Diego 30 before a holding penalty stalled them.

Following a Houston punt, Kemp started another San Diego drive late in the fourth quarter, moving the Chargers from their own 14 to the Houston 47 before a third-down pass was knocked down.

San Diego's final threat came in the closing two minutes of play. Taking over on their own 37 following a 53-yard punt by Houston's Jim Norton, the Chargers used a pass completion, a five-yard run and a pass interference penalty to move to the Oilers' 37.

With a first and 10 situation, Kemp tried to pass down the middle to his 6-feet-5-inch, 250-pound tight end Kocourek. But Houston's fine little safety, Julian Spence, who at 5 feet, 9 inches and 153 pounds was the smallest man on the field, anticipated the play, and stepped in front of Kocourek to make a game-saving interception.

Three plays later the Oilers had run out the clock to become the Champions of the American Football League for the second straight year. The game climaxed a ten-game winning streak by the Oilers.

Enough cannot be said about the amazing defensive play of both teams. San Diego had averaged 28 points a game during the season and the Oilers had averaged 36.6 points per game while becoming the only team in pro football history ever to score over 500 points during the regular season. Yet, these two high-scoring teams could manage only one touchdown and two field goals in this most memorable game.

Otto Graham

1963 Chicago Tribune Charity Game
College All Stars 20, Green Bay Packers 17

Otto E. Graham Jr. is a member of both the college and professional football Halls of Fame, but it was his prowess as a basketball player at Waukegan (Ill.) High School that enabled him to receive a scholarship at Northwestern University.

Under Coach Lynn Waldorf, Graham developed into one of the great college backs of that era and climaxed his collegiate career in 1944 when he became the only athlete ever to be named to All-America teams in both football and basketball.

When Paul Brown was handed the task of organizing the Cleveland Browns, the first player he signed was Graham. The rest is all history. Otto led the Browns to four consecutive titles in the All-America Conference and to championships and playoffs in the next six years in the NFL.

In 1958, three years after retiring as a player, Graham was invited to coach the College All Stars and defeated Detroit in a most auspicious start.

71

OTTO GRAHAM

He received a commission as commander in the Coast Guard in February 1959 and was assigned as head football coach and director of athletics at the Coast Guard Academy. He was promoted to the rank of captain on April 3, 1965.

The year 1963 was a stand-out one for Graham as a coach. Not only did his College All Stars beat one of Vince Lombardi's great Green Bay teams but the Coast Guard registered its first perfect season.

Graham returned to pro ball in 1966 as coach and general manager of the Washington Redskins, and their 7–7 record that year was the best in 10 seasons. Washington was 5–6–3 and 5–9–0 the next two seasons.

In 1970, Graham returned to the Coast Guard Academy as director of athletics.

He was born in Waukegan on December 6, 1921.

There was always great satisfaction anytime you could beat a Vince Lombardi team, but being able to defeat one of his great Green Bay teams which had won two consecutive world's championships has to be my most memorable game as a head coach.

It happened on August 2, 1963, at Soldiers' Field in Chicago, and the College All Star team I was then coaching accomplished this feat, 20-17, in the annual Chicago Tribune charity game.

This was my sixth year as coach of the All Stars. In 1958, in my very first year as the All Star coach, we defeated the Detroit Lions, but if I had any ideas that beating the defending champions would become a regular habit for the All Stars, there was a rude awakening as we lost the next four years.

Actually, when I first started to coach the All Stars, I thought, as did everyone else, that we would be completely outmatched by the best team in professional football. However, I changed my opinion drastically because I learned that the All Stars, in general terms, were just as big as the pros, just as fast and just as strong.

The one major difference was the experience advantage held by the pros. Most of their squad had played together as a unit for two, three, four years and even more, and the All Stars had only three weeks to prepare for the game.

The All Stars include the best college players in the nation. It's a squad hand-picked by the coach, and this method is better than the old way of choosing the players by popular vote.

In the years when the coach was not allowed to select his own players, the All Stars might wind up with 10 offensive linemen but none of them fast enough to be a running guard, or the team might be without a blocking back.

With the coach making his own selections, the All Stars became a well-balanced squad, capable of holding its own against the pros. In fact, I always felt that I could take any of the College All Star teams that I coached and in two or three years would have them fighting for the NFL championship.

I started to make plans for the 1963 All Star game in January of that year at the time of the annual pro draft of college players. I talked to college coaches, and I conferred a great deal with the professional scouts because, after all, knowing talent is their business. It was impossible for me to travel all over the country looking over the players myself so I relied most heavily on the judgment of the scouts.

In May, I met with my coaching staff for a couple of days. I discussed my thoughts about the squad and the game, and I set up the routine we would follow when we opened camp.

A few days before practice started in July, I met once again with my coaching staff and reviewed my plans with them.

It was not difficult preparing a game plan to use against a Lombardi-coached team because the Packers never surprised you with anything new. They did not have a varied offense or a lot of fancy plays, and you knew what to expect from their defense. Lombardi always said that you win football games because you execute the fundamentals better than your opposition. You block better than the other team, and you tackle better than they do. The Packers had good personnel, and they were well-schooled. They had beaten us 42-20 the year before, and we knew that they would come back with exactly the same offense and defense. We expected the same running plays, the same sweeps, the same pass patterns. You knew what they were going to do, and they dared you to stop them. And they dared you to run or pass against them.

When my players arrived in camp, we held a squad meeting, and I outlined our plans for the game. I told them that it was always my policy to get every player into the game, but they had to earn this right during the three weeks of practice.

I emphasized that the camp would be run like a professional football training camp. We would have rules and regulations by which they had to abide.

If they broke the rules, they, of course, could not be fined, but they would be forced to undergo what I called the "whistle" drill—a physically exhausting work-out.

Getting a squad of All Stars ready for a game in only three weeks was made somewhat easier because we had the cream of the crop on our roster.

They quickly learned our number system for designating plays. It may have differed from the system some used in college, and for a few days there was a bit of confusion from time to time, with players moving to the right when they should have gone to the left or vice versa. But because they were great athletes, they caught on very quickly.

We practiced twice a day for the first two weeks and then cut down to one daily session the final week. We worked on our running plays in the morning, and our pass plays in the afternoon.

Each session would last about 90 minutes but the coaches would stay around anywhere from 30 minutes to an hour to work with individuals on their specialties.

As I look back, I can tell you that almost without exception the players who made good in pro ball were the ones who would stay out after the regular practice and work on their specialties. The players who rushed into the dressing room the minute the practice was over were usually the ones who never made it as pros. In other words, they were not willing to pay the price, and believe me, if you don't give that extra effort and make the sacrifices, if you don't work hard at it, you won't make it because the competition is too great.

During the three weeks that we were in camp, we spent many hours showing the squad the film of the previous year's All Star game against the Packers. I think that we had allowed the Packers to score five touchdowns on passes, and most of them were cheap touchdowns. We showed them where last year's secondary had made their mistakes and kept telling them to make sure the Packers earned every point they scored this time.

As part of our practice plan, we scrimmaged against the Bears. I felt this was important since it pitted the college players against pros for the first time and they could learn that the pros were human like anyone else . . . that they block and tackle the same as anyone. If they did not have this work-out against a pro team, I was afraid that they would be somewhat awed when they took the field for the first time against the defending world's champions.

Our success in any All Star game depends upon how well our offensive line has learned the fundamentals on blocking properly for the passer, giving him the necessary protection.

Many of these linemen had not had intensive instruction on pass blocking, especially for the straight, drop-back type of passer that pro coaches prefer. For example, we knew that a lineman from a Woody Hayes team could be depended upon to block very well on running plays but would not be as effective in blocking on pass plays.

With this in mind, pass blocking was an important part of our pre-game work-outs. We spent many hours in drilling our linemen in what we call "chicken fighting." You drop back a yard and hit your man. You back up another yard and hit him again. You're slowing down the rusher. You're buying time. You're giving the quarterback three or four seconds. Maybe you can even give him five seconds. That's ample time for a passer who stays in the pocket to find his receiver.

We usually have three quarterbacks on our squad. Two, of course, would be just right if they were both healthy at game time, but if one was injured during practice and the other one hurt during the game, you might as well go home. For this game, I had picked as my quarterbacks Terry Baker, of Oregon State, the Heisman trophy winner; Glenn Griffing, of

Ole Miss; and Sonny Gibbs, of Texas Christian. Those were the three top quarterbacks in college ball during the 1962 season. However, the *Chicago Tribune* asked me if I could also add Ron Vander-Kelen, of the University of Wisconsin, to the squad as a fourth quarterback since it could mean the sale of an additional 10,000 tickets to nearby Wisconsin fans.

Ron had not enjoyed as outstanding an overall season as the other three, but had had a great game in the Rose Bowl and also did exceptionally well in the Hula Bowl. So even though I felt four quarterbacks were too many, I invited him to join the squad, and, of course, as it turned out, he was the one who won the ball game for us.

Getting a squad of football players from all sections of the country into the proper frame of mind in a short period of time isn't an easy job, but an incident that happened a week before the game seemed to give the squad a big lift.

When we issued the play books to the team, we stressed the fact that the players must be very careful because you could never tell who might get their hands on the books. In college football and pro football, nobody trusts anybody. Everybody seems to think that everyone else is the biggest thief in the world. You have to assume that the other fellow is dishonest. It's a pretty ridiculous situation, but that's the way it is.

Well, our offensive backfield coach, Tommy O'Connell, left his play book in the locker room for a minute and it mysteriously disappeared.

Some days later, I received the book in an envelope postmarked Green Bay with a note reading: "Thanks for your co-operation. We appreciate it very much." And it was signed, Vince Lombardi.

By then, I had learned that one of our players had picked up the book, given it to Ron VanderKelen, who had his mother mail it to me from her home in Green Bay.

O'Connell still wasn't aware of what had happened, and I thought that I might make good use of this incident to build up the morale of the squad.

On the Monday night before the game, I called the squad together before our only night practice and told them I had a problem. I explained that one of my coaches had committed the unpardonable blunder of losing his play book, and I didn't know what the proper punishment might be.

Without hesitation, the squad yelled: "Whistle Drill."

Well, for a couple of seconds, I didn't know what to do. At first I thought that at his age, O'Connell might have a rough time going through the physical ordeal of the whistle drill, but then when I realized that it might relieve the tension before the big game, I told them whistle drill it would be.

Everyone stormed out of the room. The players formed a circle around O'Connell, and in cadence, they had Tommy doing push-ups, sit-ups, hit-the-deck and similar exercises at a rapid pace. I thought that Tommy was going to collapse from exhaustion, but he went through it all until I called a halt after about four minutes.

Tommy came over to me, huffing and puffing, and said: "Now, let me show those so and sos. I want to give them calisthenics tonight." So after going through the whistle drill, Tommy led them in calisthenics, selecting the most gruelling exercises—the ones he knew the players disliked the most. And to the amazement of the squad and myself, he did every one of them himself.

That night you could notice the difference in the spirit among the players. You could see that the squad had been brought together as a cohesive unit, and I'm sure that this diversion from the regular routine of the camp played a part in our victory later that week.

I have never believed in the Knute Rockne type of pep talk before a game. I prefer the Paul Brown approach. In my opinion, Paul Brown is one of the truly great coaches the game has ever known. He has done more for pro football than any coach I know. He is intelligent and highly organized. He has always been the complete boss of the entire operation, and that's the only way to be successful as a coach. Brown was never the type of coach who would rant and rave at his players. If you did something to displease him, he would just look at you, and those penetrating eyes of his got across the message far more effectively than any words.

In the locker room before the kickoff, I reviewed

our game plan with the team. We thought that we would have the best chance for an effective running game by going to our weak side, with our tight end lining up on one side or the other.

This proved to be right, for we wound up with 140 yards gained on the ground. That would have been quite an accomplishment even for an experienced pro team against one of the toughest defenses in the game.

I also went over the pass plays which we thought would work well against the Packers. These were mainly short passes against members of their secondary whom we felt would be most vulnerable.

And, as I had done for three weeks, I urged the defense not to make the mistakes that we had committed the year before, when we had given them the long pass and allowed them to score one cheap touchdown after another.

I told the team to go out and play good football, execute the plays properly, get a few breaks and win the ball game. I told them to cut down on their errors and just play the type of game they were capable of playing.

VanderKelen was my starting quarterback because he had won the flip of a coin. Both he and Griffing had looked the best during the three weeks that we were in camp, and I have always followed the practice of flipping a coin whenever two or more players show up equally well at a given position.

Ron and I reviewed the first series of plays which were planned to more or less feel out the Packers.

We didn't expect them to use any new defenses against us, but we wanted to make certain. All during practice and again just before the game I told Ron and my other quarterbacks to size up the defense carefully and determine how they could key on certain personnel. "Find out which players can be trapped and run against them. If they are stronger to the left flank, run your sweeps to the right. On short passes, pick on linebackers who are not as quick as others. If a defensive back is laying back, don't throw long to that spot."

If your quarterback follows through with what you have told him . . . and the defense does what you expect it to do . . . and the quarterback throws the ball accurately, you're going to do very well and are going to be hailed as a great coach.

We kicked off to the Packers, and our defense looked strong, forcing Green Bay to punt. Boyd Dowler's kick was downed on our eight-yard line, and there are much better places from which to start your first offensive series.

On third down, halfback Larry Ferguson fumbled, and Willie Davis recovered for the Packers on our 11. Three plays later, Jim Taylor plunged over from the two, and Jerry Kramer's place kick made it 7-0.

My immediate thought was that this might be a repeat of the licking we received the previous year from the Packers, but you learn from experience that you must never get discouraged just because you fall behind early in the game.

It's always difficult playing catch-up football, but

it's not impossible. I told the players to forget it and stick in there and get the touchdown right back.

We didn't get the touchdown back, but we did manage to get on the scoreboard with a 20-yard field goal by Bob Jencks, of Miami of Ohio. Vander-Kelen moved the team well on this drive with passes to Jencks and Paul Flattery, of Northwestern, while Ferguson helped out on the ground.

Our front line continued to stop Taylor and Paul Hornung, and Bart Starr had to go to the air. He found Tom Moore open down the sideline, but Tommy Janik, a six-foot-four defensive back from Texas A & I, stepped in front of Moore and grabbed the ball. He ran it back 29 yards to the Packer 27, and we were threatening once again.

After a running play failed, VanderKelen passed to Pat Richter, of Wisconsin, who managed to out-battle three Packers for the ball on the six-yard line for a 21-yard gain. On the next play, Ferguson, be-hind some terrific blocking by tackle Bob Vogel, of Ohio State, and guard Ed Budde, of Michigan State, scored on a power play. Being able to get a touchdown by overpowering the mighty Packer line gave us a great deal of confidence. Jencks kicked the extra point, and we held a 10-7 lead with just four seconds elapsed in the second quarter.

Green Bay came back to tie the score on Kramer's 21-yard field goal, and then we missed a chance to take the lead again when Herb Adderly blocked Jencks' 19-yard field goal attempt just before the half ended.

I was pleased with our first half showing, and I told the players that if they continued to keep their mistakes to a minimum, we were going to win the game.

Our game plan was holding up because the Packers were the Packers, and they were doing exactly what we had expected them to do. Only in this game, we were executing our plays better than they were.

Although VanderKelen had called an excellent game in the first half, this being an All Star game I had to give Griffing a chance. Originally, I had intended using Griffing in the second quarter, but with Ron moving the team so well, I just couldn't take him out.

Griffing got off to a fine start in the third quarter, moving the team to two consecutive first downs, but then Adderly picked off a pass on his own 43 and ran it back 37 yards to our 20.

The Packers could gain only four yards on two plays, and on third and six, they called on Taylor to get them the first down. However, Bobby Bell, of Minnesota, Don Brum, of Purdue, and Lee Roy Jordan, of Alabama, refused to be taken out of the play and teamed up to stop Jim for no gain. Then, on fourth down, Kramer missed a 27-yard field-goal attempt.

Green Bay kept threatening, and once again we were in trouble when the Packers had a first down on our 13-yard line. We pulled out of that hole by forcing Taylor to fumble, and Danny Brabham, of Arkansas, recovered for us on the 12.

Griffing then surprised the Packers by sticking almost exclusively to a running game on a 62-yard drive. Charlie Mitchell, of Washington, helped out with an 18-yard run, and Bill Thornton, of Nebraska, gained 16 on one play, but most of it was ground out on short-yardage plays.

The Packers finally held us on the 26, and on fourth and two, Jencks booted a 33-yard field goal to give us a 13-10 lead with just under 11 minutes left in the final period.

We clung to this lead through most of the last period, but it looked like the Packers might pull it out when Elijah Pitts broke loose for a 43-yard gain. Only a fine tackle on the 17-yard line by Kermit Alexander, of UCLA, saved the touchdown.

After an incomplete pass, Fred Miller, of LSU, and Brabham nailed Pitts for an eight-yard loss. On third and 18, Starr dropped back and tossed a screen pass to Taylor, but Bell read the play perfectly and dropped Jim for a six-yard loss. Pushed back to our 31, Kramer missed a 38-yard field goal which could have tied the score.

There was 4:15 left in the game when we took over on our 20, and I had a tough decision to make. Terry Baker and Sonny Gibbs, both outstanding quarterbacks, still had not been given a chance to play. What do you do? Do you take the risk and put a cold quarterback in at this stage or do you go back to VanderKelen, who looked so great in the first half?

I didn't like the idea of violating my rule of play-

85

ing every man who has earned the right to get into the game, but I also felt that I had an obligation to the entire team and the fans.

I called Baker over, and he sensed what I was about to ask him. He was a big man about it. "Don't worry about me," he said.

So with a chance to win if we could just keep possession of the ball, I sent Ron back into the game.

Thornton gained two and Mitchell picked up four, and we were faced with a third down and four from the 26.

As always, I had allowed my quarterbacks to call most of the plays, but this was a spot where I thought I should make the decision. I called a short down-and-out pass to Richter, just long enough for the first down.

Ron hit his target perfectly on the 31-yard line, and Richter would have been stopped there if Jesse Whittenton had played him instead of the ball. But Jesse was trying for the interception, and when he failed, Richter took off and wound up with a 74-yard touchdown to sew up the game for us. Quite honestly, I felt that some of the other Green Bay secondary were loafing on the play and might have stopped Richter. Instead of rushing over and heading for Richter as soon as the ball was in the air, they just looked and watched.

Although you always take a chance whenever you put the ball in the air, I thought this particular pass was as safe as you could call. It was a simple pattern to a tall, strong receiver and would be extremely difficult to stop.

When you're faced with a third and four situation in a spot like that, you don't even consider a running play against the tough Packer line and linebackers. I would hate to try making a living that way. Sure it could be done, but you would miss many more times than you would succeed. If we had failed to make this first down, we would have been forced to kick, and with three minutes left in the game, the Packers had plenty of time to tie or beat us.

Now, with a 20-10 lead, we had it all wrapped up, and the Green Bay touchdown with six seconds left in the game didn't mean a thing.

It was my greatest victory as a coach, and many consider the game the best of the All Star games ever played.

VanderKelen and Griffing mixed their plays beautifully. We not only gained 140 yards on the ground, but VanderKelen completed nine of 11 passes for 141 yards while Griffing hit on six out of 10 for 142 yards.

Our front line allowed Taylor only 51 yards on 16 carries, and our secondary didn't give the Packers the long pass this time. We played good football all the way. We made them earn every yard they gained.

Participating in the College All Star game has always been an exciting experience for me, and I had the privilege of playing with both the All Stars and the pros before being invited to serve as coach of the All Stars.

There has been a feeling among some pro club owners and coaches that this game has outlived its usefulness and should be abandoned, but I hope this never happens.

The arguments being presented to end this annual classic just aren't sound. Sure there is a risk that a player might get hurt during the All Star game, but football is football, and a player could just as easily get hurt in his own training camp.

Then, there's the objection of players' being away from their own squad for three weeks. I know that when I was coaching the Washington Redskins, I would rather have had my players in my camp for those three weeks, but the All Star coaching staff has always been a competent one and it's always possible that the players will pick up something valuable that they might not learn from their own pro coaches.

In any event, I feel that professional football has an obligation to the College All Star game which helped the pros back in the years when they needed all the exposure they could get, and I am sure that many fans would be unhappy to see the series ended.

Sid Gillman

1964 AFL Championship Game
San Diego 51, Boston 10

Sid Gillman started his coaching career at his alma mater, Ohio State, in 1934, and with the exception of 1970, when he was sidelined because of ill health, he has not missed a season without being active as a coach.

An all-Big Ten end while at Ohio State, Gillman later became an assistant coach at Denison and Miami of Ohio and a line coach under Earl Blaik at West Point.

His first head coaching job was at Miami from 1944–47. He served in a similar post at the University of Cincinnati where his team won 50, lost 13 and tied one from 1949–54.

In 1955, Gillman became head coach of the Los Angeles Rams and led the Rams to the Western Division title in his rookie year.

When the Los Angeles Chargers were organized in 1960, he was named general manager and head coach. Gillman stayed on in that dual capacity from 1961–69 when the Chargers moved to San Diego. He served only as general manager in 1970 but returned to active coaching in 1971 when his health improved.

As coach of the Chargers, Gillman has led his teams to five Western Division crowns and one American Football League championship.

Among Gillman's former college players now coaching are Ara Parseghian of Notre Dame and Paul Dietzel of South Carolina. Two of his former players with the Rams became pro coaches—Norm Van Brocklin with Atlanta and Tom Fears with New Orleans.

Gillman was born in Minneapolis on October 26, 1911.

Many of the games that I have coached in pro football have been close, exciting ones, but the one that is my most memorable wound up one-sided.

It was San Diego's 51-10 victory over Boston on January 5, 1964, that I'll never forget because we not only won the American Football League championship but our execution that particular day was the epitome of what you expect and hope for from a ball club.

We had missed our goal of gaining the title twice in the previous three years, and each time we had felt that our team had been good enough to go all the way.

Three years before, when our franchise was still in Los Angeles, we had lost to Houston, 24-16, in the AFL championship playoffs, and two years earlier, our first year in San Diego, we were beaten once again by the Oilers, this time by a 10-3 margin.

Now, we were given our third chance in four seasons, and we came through with one of our finest efforts. In fact, that championship team was good enough to have beaten anybody in the old NFL at that time, and had the Super Bowl been started in 1965 instead of 1967, I feel the Chargers would have defeated the Chicago Bears, the NFL champions that season.

We had excellent personnel. Tobin Rote was our quarterback, and I was happy to have him with us for a few years before he decided to retire. Everyone appreciated Tobin as one of the better quarterbacks in those days. He was an outstanding talent, and I certainly enjoyed those seasons that he was with us.

Our fullback, Keith Lincoln, was as good an all-around player as any coach could want, and his running-mate in the backfield, Paul Lowe, gave us a one-two punch second to none in the league.

Complementing our running attack was a fellow named Lance Alworth, one of the all-time great pass receivers in pro football. Lance owned a pair of strong hands and rarely came out second best in fighting for the ball. He had speed and all the moves, but his greatest asset as a receiver was his ability to jump higher than any player I have ever seen. And there was no wasted motion in those leaps. Lance had the most amazing concentration and eye-hand co-ordination I have ever observed in a receiver.

It's little wonder that with such outstanding personnel, the Chargers were called the team with the most "irresistible" offense. We led the league in total offense, averaging 368 yards a game, and scored a total of 399 points in 14 regular season games.

Despite our well-balanced offense, I was worried before the championship game since Boston had given us a great deal of trouble in our two league games that season. We won the first, 17-13, and squeezed by the second, 7-6, in the lowest scoring game in AFL history.

There were some, of course, who thought that I was unduly concerned about the Patriots since we had won the Western Division title with an 11-3 record while Boston was hard pressed in tying Buffalo at 7-6-1 in the Eastern Division before capturing the playoff, 26-8.

However, I knew that I was justified in being worried about the Boston defense, which was the best in the league. The Patriots had allowed an average of 265 yards per game, giving up an average of only 79 yards a game on the ground. But more important than those figures was the fact that our explosive offense which was able to average 28 points a game could score no more than 24 points in our two games against Boston.

Lowe had been stopped cold in both these meetings. Paul, the league's second best rusher with more than 1,000 yards to his credit, could gain only six yards in the first game and nary an inch in the second one.

That's more than enough reason to forget our superior win-lose record and concentrate on coming up with something new against the tough Boston defense.

Boston's blitzing was the key to their successful defense. They employed a pressure defense, utilizing an assortment of alignments, and harassed the offense with a variety of blitzes 70 per cent of the time. I don't think that I ever saw a team that could blitz as much as they did and get away with it. They used a combination of different linebackers on their blitzes and were one of the first teams to use safety blitzes effectively.

In planning and designing an attack for this game, we had to decide between two courses of action to follow. The first was to employ a conventional, sound, safe approach to prevent any big losses and attempt to maintain possession and position by grinding out short gains. The alternative plan was to counter their hassling defense with a feast-or-famine offense. By that, I mean gambling to take an occasional big loss against long gains or touchdowns. We decided upon the latter plan.

In order to counteract their blitzes, we were determined on using a great deal of motion against them. We hoped that by putting Lincoln or Lowe in motion frequently, it would disturb Boston's system of coverage by forcing a linebacker out of position and keeping them from blitzing us the way they had in previous games. We also thought that a man in motion would make Boston more vulnerable on trap plays, and we spent considerable time working on our motion plays the week before the big game.

I did not have to say anything special to the squad in order to get them "up" for Boston. Most of the players had been in our two other championship games and were just as disappointed as I had been in our failure to win either one. Now, we had another chance, and the players did not have to be reminded about the importance of being able to go all the way this time.

We planned to use motion right from the start on our first series of offensive plays. Boston kicked off to us, and Alworth ran the ball back to our 28. Rote hit Lincoln for a 12-yard gain on a screen, and on a trap up the middle, Keith raced 56 yards to Boston's four-yard line.

On that play, we sent Lowe in motion, and Nick Buoniconti, their middle linebacker, moved out to cover him. Keith blew right up the middle, and there wasn't anyone close until Dick Felt finally tackled him.

On the next page is a diagram of that play.

Lowe picked up two yards to the 2, and Rote took it over from there. George Blair kicked the extra point, and we were in front, 7-0, after only 1:29 had been played.

The very next time we gained possession of the ball we were on the scoreboard again. With Lowe in motion to the left, Lincoln grabbed a fast toss from

Rote in the same direction, side-stepped a blitzing linebacker and raced around left end for 67 yards. In two plays, Lincoln had rushed for 123 yards, and at 2:43 of the first period, we were leading, 14-0. Our game plan was working to perfection.

On the next page is a diagram of Lincoln's touchdown run.

Boston got right back into the ball game, moving 67 yards in just seven plays. The big gainer was a 45-yard pass from Babe Parilli to Gino Cappelletti, who somehow managed to get behind Dick Westmoreland, and wasn't stopped until he reached our 10-yard line. Larry Garron gained three and then took it over from the seven, making it a 14-7 game.

Instead of collapsing after our two quick touchdowns, Boston showed it had the ability to come back. It looked like we had our work cut out for us.

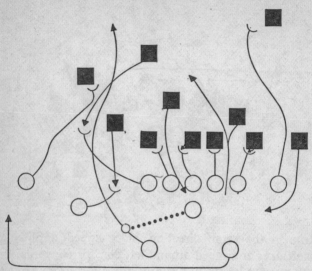

Just before the first period ended, we got that touchdown back when Lowe went 58 yards down the sidelines after taking a quick toss from Rote. Ron Mix, our 260-pound tackle, led the play, breaking Lowe loose with a key block, and then Paul outlegged the Boston secondary. I don't think that there was anybody better than Mix in leading a toss play. Despite his size, he had tremendous speed and could run the 40-yard dash in about 4.8 seconds.

On the next page is a diagram of the play.

We exchanged field goals in the second period. Blair booted one for us from the 11-yard line after we had moved 70 yards to the Boston 4, and Cappolletti kicked one from the 15 after the Patriots had marched 68 yards.

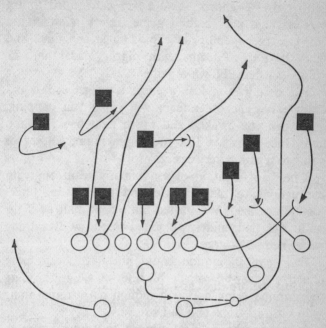

There were two minutes and 41 seconds left to play in the half when Boston scored its field goal, and I was anxious to get another score before the half ended.

We took the kick-off and in seven plays drove 71 yards, with Rote passing 14 yards to Don Norton for the score. Blair kicked the extra point, and we went into the dressing room with a 31-10 margin.

There's nothing better than to be able to take a 21-point lead into a half-time session because all you're going to do is have some fun in the locker room. Of course, we cautioned our people against getting over-confident. You never can afford to get careless in a pro football game. Every team in pro ball has the capability of exploding at any time, and there have been teams with bigger leads than 21 points that have blown a game.

The best way to lose a game is to get cocky and then relax. The other team will catch you napping, and when you awaken and try to fight back, it's too late. Once you have lost your momentum, you're not going to regain it very easily.

I had no intention of sending my team out with instructions to play it safe and protect the three-touchdown lead. We started the second half as if the score was tied, and we planned to throw everything we owned at Boston.

Our man in motion could not have been more effective against Boston's blitzing so we were going to continue using as much motion as possible along with our fast traps and fast tosses.

However, the Patriots seemed to adjust better to the motion in the third period, and we were able to score only once. That touchdown, though, was really a beauty. Mid-way in the quarter, Bob Suci barely managed to deflect a pass intended for Alworth, and Rote came right back with the same play. This time, Lance leaped high in the air, made a spectacular catch in battling Suci for the ball on the Boston 10, and broke away for the touchdown. The play covered 48 yards and gave us a 38-10 lead to take into the final period.

The game was iced in the fourth quarter when I

sent John Hadl into the game, and he managed to get us two more touchdowns. On fourth and two from the Boston 25, he passed to Lincoln, and went over from the one himself, after passing 24 and 33 yards to our tight end, Jacque MacKinnon.

Lincoln had a fantastic afternoon, carrying the ball 13 times for 206 yards, an average of 15.8. He caught seven passes for 123 yards, threw one for 20 yards and scored two touchdowns. In all, Keith's total yardage for the game was 349—a new American Football League playoff record.

Lincoln's performance overshadowed Lowe's 94 yards rushing against the team that had managed to hold him to just six yards in two games. But more important than the yards he gained was Lowe's skill in luring linebackers out of position when he was the decoy on many plays.

Between them, Lincoln and Lowe accounted for 300 of the 318 yards we rolled up on the ground.

Rote completed 10 of 15 passes, and Hadl was successful on six of 10 attempts as we gained 292 yards through the air. In all, we compiled a total of 610 yards against Boston's mighty defense.

Our own defense, led by Ernie Ladd and Earl Fazon, who could have played on any pro team in the country, held the Patriots to 75 yards on the ground and 186 yards in passing.

It was a masterful team effort, and I was proud to have been coach of a squad which will go down in history as one of the best ever to perform in pro football.

Don Shula

1965 NFL Game
Baltimore 20, Los Angeles 14

Don Shula never had a losing season during his seven years as head coach of the Baltimore Colts, but few expected that record to continue when he moved to the Miami Dolphins in 1970.

However, Shula not only had another winning season, but he had a remarkable one, winning 10 and losing four to gain the American Conference playoffs.

Shula, a halfback at John Carroll College and a defensive back for seven years with Cleveland, Baltimore and Washington, began his coaching career as an assistant for one season at the University of Virginia and then one term at Kentucky.

In 1960, he became a defensive coach for Detroit before taking on his first head coaching job at Baltimore in 1963.

His second year at Baltimore saw the Colts run up an 11-game winning streak in compiling a 12–2 mark and the Western Division title. That effort earned Shula the NFL Coach of the Year award, an honor he also won in 1968 and shared with George Allen in 1967.

Shula's '67 team was undefeated with an 11–0–2 record going into its last game against Los Angeles, and lost that one 34–10 to finish in a tie with the Rams for Division honors. However, the Rams won the right to appear in the playoffs because they had scored the most points in the two games played between the teams.

In 1968, the Colts' 13–1 mark brought them the Division and NFL crown before losing to the New York Jets in the Super Bowl.

Shula's Baltimore teams won 71 games, lost 23 and tied four in regular season play for a .755 percentage, best of any active living coach in pro ball.

Without a doubt, the December 19th, 1965, Baltimore-Los Angeles game is my most memorable one as a head coach. The week leading up to this second meeting of the year against the Rams was the strangest and most unforgettable time that I have spent in my young coaching life.

Injuries to our No. 1 quarterback and his understudy on successive Sundays created an almost unbelievable situation for me.

First, John Unitas, our great quarterback, was hurt during the Chicago Bears game. He suffered the worst type of knee injury when he was hit high and low from both sides. Our doctor gave me the unhappy news. Unitas needed immediate surgery and was out for the season.

There was still hope for us since Gary Cuozzo had done an excellent job for us earlier in the year when he was called upon to fill in for Unitas. Gary had proved his capability by throwing five touchdown passes in helping us win and keep our momentum going.

The next week against Green Bay, lightning struck again. Cuozzo was carried off the field, and I can remember how depressed I was. His injury was diagnosed as a shoulder separation which required surgery that same evening.

It was hard to believe. Two weeks and two quarterbacks lost for the season. And if this wasn't enough of a handicap before a crucial game, we had one day less to prepare for the Rams since the game was scheduled for a Saturday. My only consolation was that things couldn't get any worse.

Following Cuozzo's operation, I met with my assistant coaches in an attempt to formulate some type of game plan to present to our football team at the Tuesday morning meeting.

Here we were going into our 14th and final game of our regular season, needing a victory to stay alive in the tough Western Division. A win for Green Bay in its last game would sew up the title, but if the Packers lost, a win for us would give us the right to play the Eastern Division winners for the NFL championship. If Green Bay were held to a tie, it would mean a deadlock for first place and a special playoff game between us.

With so much riding for us on this final game, it was extremely difficult for members of our staff to mask their disappointment.

Don McCafferty, John Sandusky and Dick Bielski, our offensive coaches, wondered how they could plan an offense without a quarterback. Charley Winner and Bill Arnspager, who handled our defensive units, realized how much more would be asked of them that week.

We were an unhappy group, but we weren't going to give up without a battle. Experience had taught us a long time ago that anything could happen in sports.

My first job, of course, was to select the player to be moved into the quarterback slot. There were only two men on the squad with quarterback experience in college, and neither had been used at that position during the four or five years they had played pro ball. One was Tom Matte of Ohio State, and the other was Bobby Boyd of Oklahoma. Both their colleges had featured the running game over the pass, and whatever passing they had done was on roll-outs as opposed to the drop-back technique used by Unitas and Cuozzo.

Having worked as a running back with us, Matte was the logical choice because of his superior knowledge of our offense. I called Matte Monday evening and told him he was the man, and in typical Matte fashion he assured me he'd give it his best. At that time I wasn't aware of how good the best of Tom Matte would be.

An old friend from Pittsburgh, Art Rooney, knowing of our problem, called to let me know that Ed Brown, a veteran quarterback, was available if something could be worked out to clear him through waivers. I wanted Ed even though his value would depend on how quickly he could get with us and how much of our system he could absorb in so short a time.

On Tuesday morning I met with our squad for the first time since we lost to Green Bay, and you couldn't imagine how low their spirits were. Somehow I had to make these players realize all wasn't lost and we still had a chance to win.

The plan I presented to them that day was a simple one: play defense. Don't make any offensive errors. Work for field position and make the kicking game win for us. All I got from the players was a lot of blank stares.

It got worse when we left the meeting room and started our light Tuesday morning workout. Matte called the first play in the huddle and took his team to the line of scrimmage. To my astonishment our defensive linemen rose in unison and began to laugh. They couldn't believe Matte's high-pitched voice. It definitely lacked the command of a John Unitas.

That afternoon I received a phone call from Woody Hayes, Matte's coach at Ohio State. Woody said he had read that Tom was to be my quarterback, and he wanted to call and assure me that I didn't have anything to worry about. I told Woody I appreciated his call, but down deep I was still very concerned.

Woody said Matte would make the big play in the toughest circumstances. He ended the conversation by saying Matte's only fault as a T-formation quarterback was his inability to get the snap from the center.

So there was nothing for me to worry about— nothing except a T-quarterback who couldn't execute the simplest but most important technique.

Now I was more anxious than ever to get Ed Brown, but later that afternoon the news from Pittsburgh was far from encouraging. Acquiring Brown on waivers was not going to be as easy as anticipated.

Another club which obviously knew we were trying to get him stepped in and also claimed him, and this would mean either Pittsburgh or the Colts would have to ask the claiming club to withdraw so we could get him. I was hopeful this could be worked out but unhappy about the delay because time was more critical than ever.

Since we weren't sure of Brown, our offensive plans would have to be styled for Matte, definitely not the "pocket" type quarterback that a Brown would be. As we began our pre-game strategy, all our regular pro attack went out the window.

Normally, in preparing our game plan, we first decide on the number of offensive formations from which we want to run and pass. Sometimes we might feel that 10 to 12 sets of formations are needed in order to confuse the defense, and this requires a great deal of advance work, plus a seasoned quarterback.

Since we had neither the time nor the experienced quarterback, it was necessary to settle on a few things and attempt to do them well. Too many plays would only confuse Matte.

We decided three sets would be enough to stay simple and still give the defense enough to worry about. These are diagrams of the sets:

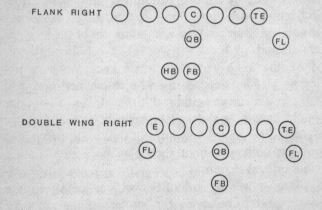

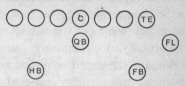

FLANK RIGHT SPLIT

We selected four basic running plays, two pass plays, plus a screen and a draw to work off each of these formations. Hopefully, this limited offense would give us some punch without putting too much pressure on Matte.

In addition to these plays, we thought Matte's running ability could be put to good use if he faked hand-offs on basic running plays and kept the ball himself. As it turned out, these "quarterback keep it" plays proved most effective.

Our practices that week resembled a high school team in its first week of fall football. Matte with the high-pitched voice, mass confusion in the huddle, uncertainty at the line of scrimmage, and finally the fumbles on the exchange from center that would stop any play before it started, did little to build my hopes.

Through it all, Matte kept his "cool." Tom had a medical history of a severe ulcer that at various times threatened to end his football career. He was constantly on medication, and if there was ever a time for it to act up, he now had a good excuse.

Looking back, I am continually amazed as to how he reacted to this intense pressure. Instead of his being the worry or "ulcer guy," he was the one who attempted to calm others. His attitude was: "Go out and give it your best shot." It was an approach which managed to give all of us confidence that somehow, someway, the best shot would be good enough.

Finally, some of the pieces began to fall in place. At times we actually resembled an offensive unit. Our four plays were being well executed, and the new quarterback-keep plays looked like they might take the Rams by surprise. There were even times when Matte managed to give a deeper pitch to his voice, and this gave us more confidence.

Before leaving for Los Angeles on Wednesday, we learned that Ed Brown had cleared waivers and would join us in California the next day. That would give him only two days to work out with us, but it was worth the effort. At this point, we would have been willing to try anything.

The minute Brown checked into our hotel, he was rushed to my suite along with Dick Szymanski, our center, and a couple of assistant coaches.

We gave Ed a list of plays that was even shorter and less confusing than the ones Matte had received. Instead of making Ed learn our numerical play calling system, each play was given a name. For example, 38 was our sweep to the right and 39 was our sweep left, but Ed would simply have to call "sweep right or sweep left," with no numbers involved.

His other running plays were: Trap, right or left; Short Trap, right or left; Dive, right or left; Fullback Slant, right or left; Fullback Draw, right or left; and Fullback or Halfback Screen, right or left.

His pass plays were limited to just two patterns. On one, he had the option of hitting the flanker on individual pattern, or the tight end on a zone pass. The second was a flood pattern to the weak side, with the flanker running an individual pattern in the event of single coverage or a "red-dog" by the defense.

He had only two formations to remember: flank and flank split.

That afternoon, Ed worked out with the team for the first time, and the "dry run" in the hotel room helped him in this first practice session. His experience was evident, and he quickly won the respect of our players.

I later learned the Rams had a "spy" watching us practice, and the fact Brown showed up kept them from concentrating too much on Matte and the type of offense he was running.

Friday, the day before the game, was devoted mostly to our kicking game, but because of our offensive predicament, we gave our "Matte offense" and our "Brown offense" one last review. The players were loose, and we all knew our title hopes were still alive.

The night before the game, our club owner, Carroll Rosenbloom, treated the squad to a dinner at one of Los Angeles' finest restaurants. The team spirit was high.

One of our players, however, missed the dinner because of a temperature and signs of the flu bug. No great concern. It was only Tom Matte.

Saturday morning at the pre-game meal Tom looked slightly under the weather but said he was ready to go. I reviewed with our quarterbacks the game plan and also the first series of plays I wanted to use.

These plays were singled out for a special purpose. We wanted to see the coverage the Rams were going to give us.

I planned to start Matte but use Brown on the second play. This was being done in order to determine at the outset if Los Angeles had planned different defensive tactics for our two new quarterbacks.

Our pre-game practice that day in the Coliseum was without a doubt the flattest and most unmoving that I have ever been associated with either as a coach or as a player. There wasn't any chatter and, more important, there was no execution. Matte, in warm up, didn't complete a pass, and Brown wasn't much better.

The pre-game practice is generally a good indication as to what to expect when the game starts, but in this instance I couldn't have been more wrong.

When we assembled in the dressing room for our last meeting before kickoff, I told the players I had never seen a worse pre-game practice, and unless our attitude changed, there would be no telling what the score might be against us.

After Don Shinnick led us in the "Lord's Prayer," a ritual with our team, I reviewed the first series of plays with the entire squad.

Then I said a final few words in an attempt to

bring the players to the positive mental outlook so necessary before taking the field.

I told them that this was the most unusual game I had ever prepared for as a coach. Many strange things had happened to us, and we were now left with our backs against the wall. Our team could go one of two ways.

We could go through the motions of playing, end the season, and not be criticized too severely because the loss of Unitas and Cuozzo gave us a built-in excuse. The other alternative was to go out and overcome all obstacles . . . refuse to be outplayed . . . hustle and hit like never before . . . and be a winner.

I reminded them that the real test of each player is what he does under adverse conditions. I urged them to reach down for that something extra to help make the big play.

It would have to be up to the defense to win the game. Our offense must not make any big errors. We would have to work for field position and rely upon our kicking game to score for us.

I finished by telling them that not many teams at this stage still had a chance to win it all, and anything could happen out there. There was no reason why they could not accomplish this upset. I told them that above all they were to enjoy every minute of the game and go home proud of the way they had played.

As we left the dressing room for the kickoff, I could feel that the team was ready to give it a great effort.

Early in the game, I was proud of the job our defense was doing on quarterback Roman Gabriel and the Rams. This was a must. Without a great defense to keep the Rams from scoring, we would face the task of trying to come from behind with an offense that wasn't capable of playing "catch-up" football.

Our defense didn't let us down. We stopped the Rams' running game and put tremendous pressure on Gabriel, sometimes with a four-man rush; other times with an all-out blitz.

Offensively, we started slowly. Our first series ended with a punt from our own 39-yard line. Later, on second and eight from the Rams' 45-yard line, I sent Brown in and he hit John Mackey on a short pass for nine yards and a first down on the 36, but the drive ended with a missed field goal from 46 yards out.

Two more series failed, and we were forced to punt from our own territory, but each time our defense held. The scoring ice was broken early in the second quarter when Lou Michaels kicked a 50-yard field goal, and we led, 3-0.

Our defense forced a fumble, and we had the ball again on the Ram 36-yard line. A running play gained eight yards, and on second and two, Lenny Moore broke off tackle and went 28 yards to score against a Ram blitz. I looked up at the scoreboard, and we led, 10-0. Hard to believe, but there it was.

You could feel our players gaining confidence and sensing they could win.

There were still 10 minutes remaining in the half,

and we were able to contain the Rams until late in the period when they climaxed an 80-yard drive with a 10-yard touchdown pass from Gabriel to Tommy McDonald. Bruce Gossett added the extra point, and the half ended with the Colts leading, 10-7.

I had nothing but praise for both our offensive and defensive units at half-time. Pleased with our three-point lead, I had no reason to change our game plan for the second half. We would continue to emphasize a ball control offense and an aggressive, swarming defense. Blitzing by the Rams was no longer a problem. They used that tactic very little after Moore's touchdown run burned them.

We expected that the Rams, after being embarrassed in the first half, would be fired up and be much tougher during the final 30 minutes.

Early in the third period Gabriel went to work on us, passing 30 yards to Jack Snow, who made the catch on our 30-yard line, out-maneuvered one of our defensive backs on the 10 and crossed the goal line to put the Rams ahead. Gossett's extra point made it 14-10.

We showed no signs of an offense during the entire third quarter, but our defense kept us in the ball game by bottling up the Rams.

The tide turned in our favor early in the fourth quarter when we came through with the big play of the game. On third down and six to go from our own 32, our spotters upstairs suggested we try to hit Mackey on a pass pattern splitting the Rams' zone defense. I sent Brown into the game with the call, and Ed tossed a perfect pass over the middle to Mackey, who out-raced two defenders and went all the way to put us out in front again. Michaels' extra point made it 17-14, Colts.

There was still plenty of time left, and now we had to keep the Rams out of field goal range since a tie would be enough to knock us out of contention for the title.

Once again our defense was superb, stopping the Rams time and again. On offense, no one could have asked more of Matte. In fact, the rest of the fourth period was almost all Matte. You would have thought that he had been our quarterback all season. A quarterback statue was good for 20 yards, and a quarterback keeper picked up 10. A quarterback draw gained 8 yards, and a quarterback bootleg fooled the Rams for 20 yards.

Not only did this ground game eat up valuable time, but it brought us close enough for Michaels to boot a 23-yard field goal to give us a 20-14 edge.

This took a little of the pressure off our defense since it meant the Rams could no longer go for the field goal.

It looked like the Rams might pull it out in the final minutes when they moved deep into our territory, but Bobby Boyd stopped the drive with an interception, and Matte ran out the clock.

We had won our impossible game. Winning is always great, but this victory had to be the greatest.

Some other glorious moments were ours that season. We faced Green Bay in the playoffs for the Western Division title and lost in a sudden-death overtime game on a disputed field goal, but we scored a devastating 35-3 victory over Dallas in the Playoff Bowl.

The Los Angeles game, however, remains foremost in my memory because each one of us stood up to be counted. We had every excuse to lose, but our team showed great character in overcoming adversity at its worst.

George Allen

1967 NFL Game
Los Angeles 34, Baltimore 10

Defense and George Allen have been synonymous during his professional football coaching career.

Beginning with his first year at Los Angeles in 1957, continuing with the Chicago Bears from 1958 to 1965, and back with the Rams from 1966 to 1970, Allen has been responsible for some of pro football's great defensive teams.

As defensive boss of the Bears, he will best be remembered for his 1963 unit which led the National Football League in 10 out of 19 categories and was second in eight others. In full appreciation for his efforts, Allen was given the game ball following the Bears' 1963 world's championship victory over the New York Giants.

When Allen moved to the Rams as head coach in 1966, he took over a team which had staggered through seven losing seasons

and brought them to a respectable 8–6
mark his first year.

In his second year, the Rams won the division crown with an 11–1–2 mark but lost to
Green Bay in the playoffs. He was named
1967 Coach of the Year by UPI, the Sporting News and the Washington Touchdown
Club, and co-Coach of the Year with Don
Shula by the AP.

In Allen's five seasons at Los Angeles, before being named coach and general manager
of the Washington Redskins, the Rams won
49, lost 17 and tied four.

Allen was graduated from the University
of Michigan in 1947 after attending Alma
College and Marquette.

He was born April 29, 1922, in Detroit.

My most memorable game as a head coach took
place in the Los Angeles Coliseum on December 15,
1967, during my second year with the Rams, and it
was a smashing 34-10 win over the previously undefeated Baltimore Colts in a battle for the Coastal
Division championship.

This was a most satisfying experience for all of us
connected with the Rams, for in just two seasons,
the team had shed its perennial losing ways and had
become one of the National Football League's pow-
erhouses.

It was a great victory, since we played almost faultless football against a team which had been rated one of the best of all time.

We will always remember this game because it marked the turning point in Roman Gabriel's career. In this, his second season as our regular quarterback, he completely out-played the fabulous Johnny Unitas, who only the week before had been named the NFL's player of the year, a well deserved honor.

Gabe hit on 18 out of 22 passes for 257 yards and three touchdowns. It was one of the finest passing performances that we have ever seen and gave him the necessary confidence to go on and become one of the top quarterbacks in the business.

Our victory prevented the Colts from becoming the first pro team in the last 25 years to finish its season unbeaten. Up until this final game of the regular season, Baltimore had won 12 games and tied one. That deadlock was a 24-24 contest with us earlier in the season.

We entered the big game against Baltimore with the best record in Ram history. After taking all six of our pre-season games, we had won 11, lost one and tied one, yet we were trailing the amazing Colts by one full game. Our one defeat was at the hands of San Francisco by a 27-24 margin, on a last-quarter 28-yard touchdown pass from John Brodie to Sonny Randle.

Ordinarily, you can lose two or three games and still win your Division title, but we had the misfortune of compiling our great record at a time when the Colts were red hot.

The pressure on us kept mounting as the season went along. Playing on the West Coast, three hours later than in the East, we often would know the outcome of the Baltimore game before our kickoff. Sometimes this could be an advantage, but during the 1967 season, it simply put more and more pressure on us because week after week, Baltimore kept winning.

That meant we had to win in order to stay in the race. One more loss or a tie, and it could be all over for us. We were in a pressure cooker most of that season. It was really rough on our players.

Only once had we been able to put a bit of pressure on the Colts. It was the week prior to our final game when we faced the Green Bay Packers in the Coliseum in a Saturday afternoon game.

The Green Bay game was televised, and the Baltimore players were able to watch it back home. This Green Bay game turned out to be one of the most famous in Ram history. The Packers were leading by four points, 24-20, had possession on their own 47-yard line with only 54 seconds on the clock when they were forced into a punting situation. The punt block rush was on, and Tony Guillory broke through the middle to block Donnie Anderson's kick. Claude Crabb picked up the loose ball and returned it to the Green Bay five-yard line.

With just 37 seconds left, Gabriel threw a pass into the corner of the end zone to Bernie Casey for the game-winning touchdown, and we stayed alive in the Coastal Division race.

The Colts, of course, were rooting for the Packers to win since it would give the Colts the title, and some of the Baltimore players later said that they felt like they had been in a ball game themselves instead of just watching us.

The emotional side of football cannot be stressed enough. Sure we all know that the physical and technical end of the game is important, but unless the players have the proper mental attitude, they won't win consistently.

We tell our players that every day is a big day. No day should go by without accomplishing something. Waste a day and you wind up feeling sorry for yourself.

It is extremely difficult to keep individuals highly motivated day after day, week after week, but the most successful athletes are those who can stay motivated.

We had no problem getting the Rams fired up for the Colt game. This contest had been building up for a long time. It was our championship game. It was our Super Bowl.

The long season had now boiled down to the final 60 minutes. We could not afford another tie. It was all or nothing. By winning, the Rams would finish tied for first place but would be declared the Division champions under a ruling that the team scoring the most points against the other takes the title.

In order to win, we had to stop Unitas. A big rush

was needed from our front four. Give Unitas time, and he will thread a needle. He had too many outstanding receivers to help him. John Mackey had already proven that he was the best tight end in modern football. Ray Berry's record spoke for itself. Willie Richardson was as fast as they come. Lenny Moore always seemed to make the big play. Tom Matte was always dangerous in the clutch. The Colt line was outstanding.

So we felt that the only way to stop Unitas was to keep the pressure on him and not allow him to get set. It's one thing to plan a big rush and another thing to execute it properly. In 13 previous games, Unitas received such excellent protection that he was sacked only 18 times. That's an average of 1.4 times per game. Unless we could do better, we would be in trouble.

Our front four did perform better . . . much better, breaking through to dump Unitas no less than seven times. Their rush was so great that Unitas frequently had to unload his passes too quickly. Two were intercepted.

In our offensive game plan, we also were concerned about Baltimore's rush. Their front four and three linebackers could kill you. They shift around and red dog a great deal. We had to be ready to pick up the dogs.

It would be necessary for Gabe to read their defenses and call a few audibles. He would have to pick apart their zone defense which the Colts used so effectively.

121

Against the zone, Gabe would need to concentrate on hitting his targets either between their defensive backs or in front of them. The pass patterns run by the receivers would be most important.

Those were the two big things we worked on all week; on defense, a big rush against Unitas; on offense, pass patterns that would wreck their zone.

We had a short meeting in the dressing room before we took the field against the Colts. I don't believe in long sessions. Ours usually last about five minutes. In that time, we briefly review what we have done all week.

It is my feeling that a review of what we have planned is easily absorbed in that "waiting" period prior to the game and helps everyone to use the time to the fullest advantage.

I met with the defensive "generals," and we discussed Unitas and his dangerous passes to Matte and Moore and what our counters were against them. We reviewed the defenses we felt were the most effective for this game, and there was a special feeling of urgency among Maxie Baughan and the other signal callers. You could feel the concentration in their answers and questions. We felt that the defense was going to play a "great game," and everyone was prepared and ready.

I then went to meet with Roman Gabriel and found him in the same apprehensive mood and, in going over the offensive game plan with him, noted that he had a true grasp of what we planned to do to move the ball against the outstanding Colt defense. There was no doubt that he was ready to lead the offense to a top effort.

Now it was time for the "early birds" (kickers and special team members) to leave to go out to warm up. It was actually eight minutes earlier than scheduled time to leave, but I felt they had to be turned loose. I got them together at the door to the dressing room, and all I had to say was: "You know what we came here to do today! Now let's go out and start doing it."

They practically ran me and the dressing room doors down as they headed out the long ramp to the field. I was convinced we were going to play a RAM game.

We took the opening kickoff and quickly moved into Baltimore territory, but Dick Bass fumbled on the 25 and the Colts recovered.

In just a few minutes, we had the ball back, and this time we got on the score board as Bruce Gossett booted a 47-yard field goal.

Our lead, however, was short lived. Sideline passes by Unitas, combined with plunges by Tom Matte and Tony Lorick, brought the ball from the Colts' 35 to our 12 from where Unitas passed to Richardson in the end zone for the score. Willie made a great diving catch, and we trailed 7-3, with just seven seconds left in the period.

Early in the second quarter, Lou Michaels missed a 37-yard field goal, and then we caught the Colts by surprise. On the first play from our own 20, Gabe decided to try a long pass against the zone after

Jack Snow had reported that Al Haymond, their defensive corner back, had been playing him tight at the line of scrimmage.

Jack felt that he could get free deep so Gabe called a play originally designed for Bernie Casey on a short pattern, hoping the Colts would stay in their same defense.

They did. Gabe faked a handoff to Les Josephson as Snow ran straight ahead for 12 yards and then turned on the steam as he crossed over to the middle.

He got behind Rick Volk and Bobby Boyd, gathered in the pass on the Baltimore 36 and raced into the end zone untouched. It was a beautiful call, perfectly executed, and gave us a lead which we never relinquished.

We did have some uneasy moments later in the period when the Colts drove from their own 33 to our 23. Unitas was moving the team well, and we were in trouble. If they couldn't go all the way, they were close enough for a field goal which would tie the game.

On second and six, Unitas tried to hit Moore on a play which could have put the Colts in front, but Eddie Meader intercepted the pass and the threat was erased.

That definitely was the turning point of the game. It ended a serious Baltimore threat and then spurred us on to another score. Starting from our own 19, Gabe moved us 81 yards in nine plays.

The scoring play came on a 23-yard pass to Casey

with just 10 seconds left in the half. The Colts were in one of their rare man-to-man defenses and had a safety blitz going. This is usually a good spot for a draw, but Gabe had confidence in his offensive line and did not call an audible.

Our line was invincible, and the safety could not get through. Casey faked his man, Haymond, to the inside and then headed for the corner of the end zone. Gabe's pass was right on the button, and Bernie grabbed it just a step or two in bounds.

We left the field with a 17-7 lead and were confident of victory.

In the dressing room for the half-time meeting, I gathered the complete defense together, and in going over the tendencies we had faced in the first half, we noted that the game plan was right on the button. We discussed the possible changes we might expect from the Colts' offense, but we knew if we could keep our domination over them for another 30 minutes, we would have one of the great victories in Ram history and of our lives.

There was no feeling of "a job well done," since we knew how the Colts would explode if you let up for even a minute.

The official came into the dressing room to notify us of the five-minute warning to return to the field, and now we began our meeting with the offense. The most effective plays were reviewed, and the offensive game plan was holding up the way we had expected.

There was no reason to remind them again of

what we had to do, as the players themselves were doing that to each other.

We had been a fine second-half team all season long, and all I had to say was: "Alright, now let's go out there and show them how the RAMS play ball in the second half, and we'll come back to these dressing rooms with the win we came here to get."

As they exploded toward the doors I knew there was no complacency among us. Offense, defense and special teams were ready to get the job done. The 40-man team was on its way to the field.

Our front four never eased up a minute on Unitas in the second half. Passing from his own 25, John barely did get the ball off, but it would have been better to have eaten it. Jack Pardee picked it off for us at mid-field and ran it back to the Colts' 21. We were forced to settle for Gossett's 23-yard field goal, but the way we were playing, the 20-7 lead looked very good.

We found ourselves on defense for all but four plays during the remaining nine and a half minutes of the third period. Unitas was having his troubles against our big rush, but managed to sustain one long drive by coming through three times on crucial third-down plays.

When he picked up a first down on our 14, our defense stiffened. Matte and Lorick each gained two yards, making it third and six from the 10. Unitas tried to cross us up on a quarterback draw instead of a pass, but we were waiting for him. He made only four, and it was now fourth and two from the six.

At this point, the Colts showed great respect for

our defense by electing to go for the field goal. Lou Michaels booted it on the first play of the fourth period, cutting our lead to 20-10.

The Colts never threatened after that. We completely demoralized them by taking the ensuing kickoff and going 67 yards in just seven plays. Gabe set it up with passes to Tommy Mason, Bill Truax and Casey. Then, on second and seven from the Colts' nine-yard line, he sent Casey into the corner of the end zone as the primary receiver but spotted Truax open in the middle. He fired a strike to Bill, and we had a 27-10 lead with 11:15 left in the game.

Our last touchdown was a gift in the final minutes. Back to pass on a fourth and 13 situation from his own 12, Unitas was dropped for an eight-yard loss. Dick Bass took it over from the two, and we had crushed the favored Colts, 34-10.

It was a magnificent team effort on our part. Gabe could not have been better in out-duelling Unitas, but this was not a one-man show. You need the protection; you need the receivers; you need the defense; and you need the kicking team.

To win a game like this, you need an all-out team effort, and that's exactly what we received.

Tom Fears

1967 AFL Game
New Orleans 27, Atlanta 24

Tom Fears has been coaching professional football since 1959 when he became an assistant to Vince Lombardi at Green Bay.

He left the following season to aid his old teammate, Bob Waterfield, who had become head coach of the Los Angeles Rams, but returned to Green Bay in 1962 to help Lombardi coach the Packers to the world's championship.

Fears was still with the Packers in 1965 when they won the title again but moved on to Atlanta the following year to become chief offensive coach for the newly organized Falcons.

In 1967, he was named head coach of another expansion team, the New Orleans Saints, and in his three seasons with the newest franchise in the National Conference, his teams finished with 3–10, 4–9–1 and 5–9 records—the best achievement of any expansion team in pro football history.

128

He was relieved as head coach during the 1970 season and was signed as an assistant coach for the 1971 season by the Philadelphia Eagles.

During World War II, Fears captained the Second Air Force Superbombers and upon his discharge entered UCLA where, in 1947, he was captain, All-American end and most valuable player in the Rose Bowl.

In nine seasons with the Los Angeles Rams, Fears caught 400 passes, including a record-breaking 84 in 1950, and has been named to Pro-Football's Hall of Fame.

Fears was born in Los Angeles on December 3, 1923.

I was feeling a little downhearted 10 games deep into the 1967 season, my first as a head coach and the first for the newly formed New Orleans Saints.

We had been able to win only one game while losing nine, and our next opponent was the Atlanta Falcons, whose record was one victory, eight defeats and one tie.

Feeling the grinding pressures of a long and trying season, I dubbed the game, "the Cellar Bowl," but it really was for the championship of Dixie. And, it was played that way.

I wanted to win badly because it was our final home game of the season, and our fans and players needed a victory to lift their spirits. Then, too, I had spent the previous season at Atlanta as an assistant to Head Coach Norb Hecker, and football men always want to beat their former teams.

In addition, we had planned a program after the game—win or lose—so that we could pay tribute to our fans for their unfaltering support. All week long I thought about how terrible it would be to lose and then have to go through with the program.

Our opponents weren't taking us lightly even though we were a first-year term. The Saints won five out of six pre-season games, and other coaches sat up and took notice.

Rival coaches were determined not to lose to New Orleans. They felt that you could not offer much of an excuse for losing to a first-year expansion club.

I'm an authority on expansion clubs. I was with the Atlanta Falcons when they were first formed, and then I moved over to New Orleans. Coaches of established teams have a multitude of problems, but they are nothing compared to those of a coach with an expansion team.

You have to work with players no other team wants and with rookies you pick up in the regular draft. The established teams protect their 29 best players before they let you get a crack at their 30th player. Then, you don't even know if you are getting the 30th best. It might be their 37th best or even their 40th.

You never get wealthy or healthy from the expansion draft. In most cases, the players made available to you have a problem of some type, and you are fortunate if they perform any better for you. Considering our personnel of cast-offs and rookies, it had to be a humiliating experience for an established team to lose or even be tied by an expansion club.

As it turned out, we wound up winning three games our first year, and those victories were accomplished against three great quarterbacks—Norman Snead of Philadelphia, Randy Johnson of Atlanta, and Sonny Jurgensen of Washington. This was regarded as an excellent showing for an expansion team as compared to some of the others before us. Dallas, for example, couldn't even get a tie game until the final game of its first season.

One thing that helped us that first year was the tremendous support of our fans. They backed us nobly, with much devotion and perseverance. They had come back week after week, more charged up than the week before, to support the Saints.

This phenomenal dedication influenced our squad. The players could feel the spirit the fans had in the stands. It was almost something you could physically reach out and grab. It was in the air, and it caused the adrenalin to move in the most unemotional of our players. It infected the players to such an extent that they continually came through with extra effort performances.

You can't win on enthusiasm alone, but on occasion, you can beat a better team when given the proper breaks and the kind of rabid encouragement the New Orleans fans provided for the Saints.

Mainly because of the "never-say-die" attitude of our fans and the manner in which the Saints responded, I'll never forget Sunday, November 26, 1967. Neither will the 83,400 fans who packed Tulane Stadium.

Blitzing was to be an important part of our defense against Randy Johnson since I felt that any young, inexperienced quarterback would become flustered, the more problems you give him.

However, we made one mistake after another as Atlanta took the opening kickoff and moved down to our 10-yard line. Our defense was ragged, but we received a break when Ron Rector fumbled and Bill Cody recovered for us.

Later in the quarter, Gary Cuozzo went to work on Atlanta's zone defense, and four passes—two to Ernie Wheelwright and two to Danny Ambramowicz—helped take us to the Falcons' 12. A clipping penalty pushed us back to the 27. Cuozzo tried three passes and missed on each one, but we got on the scoreboard with Charlie Durkee's 34-yard field goal at 11:41 of the first quarter.

That lead was short lived as the Falcons took the kickoff and went 80 yards in 10 plays. We weren't hitting, and nothing was going right for us. Johnson, passing from our 20-yard line, lofted the ball to his split end, Jerry Simmons, in the end zone, and our safety, George Rose, was called for interference. Junior Coffey went over from the one for the touchdown, and with less than a minute of the second quarter gone by, the Falcons were in front, 7-3.

Moments later, Wheelwright fumbled after catching a screen pass, and Joe Szczecko recovered for the Falcons on our 32. Johnson pitched out to running back Perry Lee Dunn, who faked a sweep and then passed to Tommy McDonald in the end zone. The play failed to fool our secondary, and we had two men covering McDonald all the way. I thought we were going to have an interception, but the ball glanced off the chest of one of our men, and McDonald made an easy catch. Atlanta led, 14-3, and it looked bad for New Orleans.

We continued to make mistakes. Cuozzo passed 22 yards to wide receiver Ray Poage, but when the ball came down hard against his knee, Ray fumbled. The ball bounced into the air and was grabbed by Jerry Richardson, who ran it back to our 21.

Five plays later, Johnson hit tight end Billy Martin with a five-yard pass in the end zone on a square out pattern, and we were trailing, 21-3. It appeared as if our world was caving in.

However, just before the half ended, we cut the margin to 21-10 as Cuozzo passed seven yards to tight end Kent Kramer under the goal posts. That touchdown pumped some new life into us, and I felt better going into the dressing room.

During the half-time break, I finally decided to replace Cuozzo at quarterback with Billy Kilmer. Mid-way in the second quarter, when we were behind, 21-3, I was planning on using Kilmer in the second half, but when Cuozzo got us the touchdown, I wasn't too sure about making the change.

I considered a number of factors, and then gave the nod to Kilmer. Atlanta had been blitzing us more than they had shown a tendency to do earlier in the year, and with the type of protection we were able to give the passer at that time, Cuozzo was not as well suited to the blitz as Kilmer.

Kilmer wasn't any more mobile than Cuozzo, but when he was racked up, Billy never seemed bothered and would come back as though nothing happened.

I also thought that Kilmer might give us the necessary spark in the second half. We had given our players psychological tests before the season, and the psychologist told me that as far as valor was concerned, Billy would have been one great kamikaze pilot.

He was so cool under pressure that if we were sitting in a building that started to shake during an earthquake, he would sit right there with you and talk the whole thing out while others would panic.

My only instructions to him was to establish a running game to make our passing more effective.

Despite the touchdown we scored late in the second quarter, I was disappointed with the overall performance of our team, and I told them in no uncertain terms that they were playing like Ned in the Third Reader. Atlanta wasn't beating us. We were beating ourselves with one mistake after another. We would have to buckle down and play better football in the second half.

Atlanta kicked off to us, and it was a short one giving us excellent field position. We started a drive on our own 47 and Jim Taylor's running, combined with some effective passing by Kilmer, moved us to Atlanta's 22 in four plays.

I sent Taylor's back-up man, Randy Schultz, into the game, and Kilmer called for an off-tackle play. However, Randy spotted a big hole over the middle, and he ran to daylight.

Although bothered by a pulled leg muscle which reduced much of his power, Schultz managed to zig-zag his way past the Atlanta secondary. Sam Williams, the Falcons' defensive end, almost nailed him just beyond the line of scrimmage, but Randy spun away and then helped by two tremendous blocks by Ray Rissmiller and Kent Kramer, he scored at 3:12 of the third quarter to cut Atlanta's lead to 21-17.

Later in the period, we drove to the Atlanta 20, but Durkee's 27-yard field goal attempt was off to the left. Durkee did come through for us during the early part of the fourth quarter with a 32-yard boot, and now we trailed by only one. Another field goal could win it for us, but Atlanta eliminated that possibility when Wade Trayham kicked a 26-yard goal with 4:25 left in the game.

Time was now an important factor. Atlanta's kickoff was taken by Don McCall, a fearless rookie, on our own five, and he was knocked back to the three. We had 97 yards to go, but from the way our fans were cheering for us, you'd have thought we were getting ready to score.

Wheelwright, a big running back we had obtained

135

from Atlanta in September, made only two yards on an end sweep, but we wound up on the 20 when the Falcons committed a personal foul.

Kilmer hit wide receiver John Gilliam with a perfect 35-yard pass down the middle. John made a great catch with two defenders around him.

Kilmer figured that the Falcons would remain vulnerable down the middle since they were double teaming Dan Ambramowicz and Walt "Flea" Roberts on the wings.

He again threw over the middle, this time to Ray Poage, who made a leaping catch on the Atlanta 27. Then, with the Falcons lined up in anticipation of another pass, we called a draw, and Tom Barrington went 14 yards for a first down on the 13.

There were two minutes and 23 seconds left, and time no longer was so vital a factor. Barrington picked up a yard around end, and figuring that Atlanta was again expecting a pass, we tried to cross them up with another draw. This time they weren't fooled, and Schultz was dropped for a five-yard loss.

It was third and 14, and now we had to pass. Kilmer's toss to Ambramowicz was batted down. Time might not have been a factor, but now we were running out of downs. We faced a do-or-die fourth down play from the 17-yard line, and the roar from the crowd was deafening.

Kilmer sent wide receiver Roberts down deep, and it looked like we had reached the end of the road when the pass was intercepted by Ken Reaves in the end zone.

However, the officials had caught Atlanta's Richardson bumping Roberts on the seven-yard line, and the Falcons were charged with pass interference.

Kilmer later said that he figured that he could hang the ball up there and let the speedy Roberts run under it. Roberts was hit while the ball was in the air, and thank goodness there was an official close by to spot the infraction.

We now had another opportunity, with a first down on the seven. The clock showed 1:02 to play.

Wheelwright was stopped cold at the line of scrimmage, and only 58 seconds remained.

On a play-action pass, Kilmer looked for Ambramowicz, his primary receiver, but Dan was well covered. Billy then spotted Kramer about three yards deep in the end zone. A defensive back was at Kramer's right shoulder so Kilmer fired the pass to the left side.

The ball couldn't have been thrown any better, but Kramer was forced to make a spectacular one-handed catch. (He later explained that someone was holding his other hand.)

Cannons boomed, and the 83,400 fans went wild. The noise in the Stadium was deafening. We had erased Atlanta's 24-20 lead, and victory was ours—if only we could hold the Falcons.

There were only about 40 seconds left, but in a game like this, anything could happen. Hecker and the Falcons wanted this game as much as we did.

We set our defenses to protect against the bomb. We were willing to give Atlanta the short passes, knowing the clock was in our favor.

Our plan was working fine, and there were only seconds left in the game when Johnson dropped back on what we figured had to be the final play. Everyone in the Stadium knew that this was going to be a long, desperation pass, and we were right. Johnson aimed his bomb at Jerry Simmons, his wide receiver who had been with us during our pre-season games.

Simmons somehow managed to get open at our 25-yard line, and I was almost afraid to look as I saw the ball sailing towards him. But miraculously, the ball rolled off his fingertips. Time had run out, and we won 27-24.

It was a Hollywood finish. It was the sweetest of victories because of our gallant comeback. What a way to wind up our home schedule!

Then something rare in professional football happened. The crowd stayed on for at least 45 minutes.

The players lined up across the field, one sideline to the other. Several players, owner John W. Mecom, Jr., and I each said a few words of heartfelt appreciation to the fans for the loyal and unbelievable support they had given us throughout our first season.

Guard Eli Strand, captain of our special teams, stood at the field microphone and told the people: "I've played in a lot of towns, and I've seen a lot of fans, but folks, believe me, I've never seen any fans anywhere like you. You're the greatest!"

Tears were streaming down Eli's face. Ernie Wheelwright was sobbing like a child.

The fans cheered again and again.

Then, each of the players was introduced for the final time of the 1967 season, some for the last time ever. Each player trotted off the field between a corridor of cheerleaders. And still the fans stood and roared their approval.

Finally, the band played Auld Lang Syne. Some of the crowd sang along. Others stood with tears in their eyes.

It was a heart-tugging moment that occurs too rarely in football. I had never seen anything like this in my many years as a player and coach. It was little wonder that I had a lump in my throat.

When I left the dressing room later that afternoon, there was still a sprinkling of fans in the stadium.

All of the ingredients were there that afternoon for a Hollywood script, but the film-makers would never buy it. They would say it was much too unreal!

Hank Stram

1970 Super Bowl
Kansas City 23, Minnesota 7

Henry "Hank" Stram spent 12 years as an assistant coach for four different college teams, but once he entered the professional ranks as a head coach, he has stayed with the same club.

In 1960, when LaMar Hunt founded the American Football League, he organized the Dallas Texans and picked Stram as his coach. Now the Kansas City Chiefs, the team has known no other leader.

After his 1948 graduation from Purdue, where he won the Big Ten Medal for best combining athletics with scholarship, Stram stayed on with the Boilermakers as backfield coach for eight years. Hank moved to Southern Methodist in 1956 for one season, then spent two years at Notre Dame and one at Miami (Fla.).

In the pro ranks, Stram has led his teams to three American League championships. In 1962, when the Chiefs were the Dallas Texans, they defeated Houston, 20–17, in the longest football game ever played (77 minutes and 54 seconds of a six-quarter overtime contest). In 1966, as the Chiefs, they played in the first Super Bowl against Green Bay, and in January 1970, after winning their third crown, the Chiefs defeated Minnesota in the fourth Super Bowl.

Stram was named Coach of the Year in 1962, 1966, 1968 and 1969 by a number of organizations. Following his Super Bowl victory, the New York chapter of the Football Writers' Association chose Stram as their Super Man of the Year.

If I had been asked before January 11, 1970, to select my most memorable game as a pro coach, I would have chosen the 1962 American Football League Championship which was the first league title of my career. As the Dallas Texans we defeated the defending champion Houston Oilers, 20-17, after 15 minutes and 54 seconds of sudden-death overtime. For sheer excitement, tension, and drama that game is difficult to match. We had a 17-0 half-time lead, but they tied the score in the second half. Tommy Brooker's 25-yard field goal finally gave us the victory in the longest professional football game ever played.

I also would have given consideration to our 1967 appearance in the first Super Bowl game, even though we lost to Green Bay 35-10.

That game rates among my most memorable ones for a number of reasons. First, I felt it was a great honor to be the first American Football League representative in the Super Bowl. I had been in the league since its inception in 1960, and we had been looking forward to opposing the NFL champions for some time. There was further significance in the fact that LaMar Hunt, our club owner, was the founder of the AFL, and it was a great challenge for all of us to be playing against Green Bay, then the glamour team of professional football and one of the best pro teams in a long, long time.

Even though I will always reserve a special place in my memories for these two games, they have to make room for the 1970 Super Bowl in New Orleans where we defeated the Minnesota Vikings, 23-7, for the world championship of professional football.

The year before, the New York Jets had become the first American Football League team to win the Super Bowl by beating Baltimore, 16-7, but there were still quite a few football fans who were skeptical about that win by the Jets.

Certainly the oddsmakers were foremost among the disbelievers.

As a coach, you don't pay much attention to the odds listed in the newspapers, although you can't help but be aware of them. I thought it was peculiar that even before the oddsmakers had known the opposing teams in the 1970 Super Bowl, the NFL was made a 13- or 14-point favorite, which meant to me that they were still basing their judgments on leagues instead of people.

That's a mistake some people have been making since the inception of our league. I feel very strongly about the fact that pro football is not a game of insignias, nor is it a game of leagues. It is a game of people, and as a result it was hard for me to understand how anyone could justifiably say that one team was going to be a 13-point underdog because of its league.

However, I think we made believers out of most of them. We entered the game as a very confident football team. We had grown considerably since the first Super Bowl game, and developed greatly as far as maturity, poise, and confidence are concerned.

I think that we all relate to experiences, and the fact that we could relate to a Super Bowl experience, even though we didn't succeed, helped us immeasurably.

During the week prior to the Super Bowl, I was very upset with the way our quarterback, Len Dawson, had been linked unfairly to a gambling investigation. It was a very irresponsible charge, and created some anxious and trying hours. It put great pressure on Lennie, much more so on him than it did our squad and staff. This kind of thing could work against or be an advantage to a team. It would certainly be a big burden on a young team, but ours was not a young team emotionally; and Lennie responds to pressure

143

and adversity as well as any player I have ever coached. Because of my great confidence in Lennie and our entire squad and because of the many adversities we had overcome during the season, I didn't think this would really be a problem.

I told our squad before we started the season that anytime a group of 40 people work for six months to achieve a goal, there is bound to be adversity, but we had to be strong enough to overcome these adversities and continue to win.

For example, we lost Dawson for six games and then we lost our back-up quarterback, Jackie Lee, because of injuries. I told the squad that we couldn't insulate ourselves with a reason to fail just because of an injury. We would still have to find a way to win. As a result, the team rallied around each other, maintained a great feeling of confidence and poise and continued to play with a strong purpose . . . to win. The maturity with which we reacted during the season carried over to this game.

When the story on Dawson broke, we had that same feeling of confidence; and even though there was concern among all of us, I thought it was important for us to clear the air so that we could concentrate all of our attention and efforts on the game. We did just that by calling a press conference.

The press conference cleared the air, and we worked and prepared without any ill effects.

Part of our pre-game practice was, of course, devoted to working out a plan to stop Joe Kapp. We thought it was important to keep Kapp in the pocket as much as we could. Looking at the films it became very evident to us that he could move by design and throw on the run as well as anyone we had seen all year.

We decided to use our triple stack defense, which is an over-shifted defense to the strong side. Structurally speaking, the defense is one whereby we move our defensive ends, Jerry Mays and Aaron Brown, from the inside position of the tight end to a position outside the tight end. We call this our odd spacing which means that we would have Buck Buchanan or Curley Culp on the nose of their center, Mick Tinglehoff. We hoped that these two aspects of our defensive approach to the game would prevent Kapp from doing an effective job on his rollouts, and they did. Although Kapp completed 16 of 25 passes, most were fairly short. He ran only twice for a total of nine yards, and he has dropped three times for a total of 21 yards in losses.

We felt that Minnesota's tight end would hurt us more than their outside receivers, since we are basically a zone defense team and use that type of coverage most of the time. We were right about that as their great receiver, Gene Washington, caught only one pass and that one for only nine yards. He was so well covered that they threw to him only three times all afternoon.

Our offensive game plan was a fairly simple one. We thought that it was very important to double team both defensive ends on all of our short passing attempts. This was something we had never done before, but we knew their cornerbacks played a little soft, and we wanted to throw in front of them and throw quickly so that they would not disturb the flight of the ball.

We were aware that their defensive ends had great range and were good leapers. We knew that if we did not double team them, there was a danger of the ends' knocking the ball down.

We also double teamed them on all of the off-tackle plays and on plays we ran right at them. We wanted to run directly at them because they read plays, reacted, and pursued as well as anybody we had seen.

We also wanted to use some mis-direction plays. We used a variety of end-around plays from different formations during the regular season, but the ones we used so successfully against Minnesota were plays we hadn't used too much before. Oddly enough, these end-arounds which turned out so well for us in the Super Bowl weren't too successful during the season.

We decided to go on a quick count because it would change the tempo of the Minnesota defense. We ran on quick counts 27 times during the game, and this was very effective.

We used 17 different offensive formations, but basically we did not deviate too much from the approach we had used all year. For example, we used 21 formations against Oakland.

I was hoping that we would win the toss and get a chance to get on the scoreboard first, but we lost and kicked off to Minnesota. Kapp moved his team well, and the Vikings went from their own 20 to our 39 where we held. On fourth down, with the wind against them, Minnesota decided to punt instead of trying for the field goal, and we went on the offensive for the first time.

We were able to advance to Minnesota's 41 where the Vikings' defense stiffened. Jan Stenerud kicked a Super Bowl record 48-yard field goal, which gave us a 3-0 lead with a little over eight minutes gone in the first quarter.

Late in the first quarter, we started a drive from our own 20 and moved 55 yards to Minnesota's 25 where we were stopped. Stenerud was called on again and came through with a 32-yard field goal to give us a 6-0 lead with 13:20 left in the half.

It wasn't too much later that we got another drive going, and helped by a 19-yard run by Frank Pitts on a flanker reverse, we were able to get down to the Minnesota 18.

Once again, we were unable to go all the way, and this time Stenerud kicked a 25-yard field goal to increase our lead to 9-0 with 7:52 left in the half.

On the ensuing kickoff, Charley West fumbled the ball, and Remi Prudhomme recovered for us on the Minnesota 19.

Dawson went right to work, trying to get us our first touchdown, but he was thrown for an eight-yard loss attempting to pass. On a quick count, quick opening play from the I formation, Wendell Hayes picked up 13 yards. Dawson rolled out to the right and passed to flanker Otis Taylor down the right sideline for 10 yards and a first down on the four.

Mike Garrett lost a yard and then was stopped at the line of scrimmage. On third down, Garrett went over from the five on what we called our 65 toss power trap.

On this play, our left tackle, Jim Tyrer, pulled to influence his man, Alan Page. Page came through, and our right guard, Mo Moorman, pulled and took him out of the play with an inside-out trap block. Our tight end, Fred Arbanas, took care of their middle linebacker, enabling Garrett to score off-tackle after taking a short pitch from Dawson.

Stenerud's extra point made it 16-0 at 9:26 of the period, and that's the way the score remained the rest of the half.

During half-time, I told our squad that we had been working toward this goal since we first started our pre-season weight lifting program back in March. Now it boiled down to just 30 more minutes, and the remaining 30 minutes of the game would probably be the most important minutes of our lives—and nobody was going to take it away from us.

Even though we had a 16-0 lead and had moved the ball well in the first half, we were concerned about the second half since we had seen how Minnesota had been able to come back against the Los Angeles Rams.

We left the dressing room at half-time with the idea of not being conservative. We felt we could not sit on our 16-0 lead. We wanted to stay on the offensive. We were going to throw the ball and continue to do the things that we thought we could do going into the game.

We received the second half kickoff and had possession of the ball for the first six minutes but couldn't get another score.

When Minnesota took over on their own 31, they moved 60 yards in 10 plays, with Dave Osborn going over from the four. Fred Cox added the extra point to cut our lead down to 16-7 at 10:28 of the third period.

Kapp had looked especially good during the drive as he passed to John Beasley for 15, Bill Brown for 11, and finally to Oscar Reed for 12 and a first down on our four.

We knew that Minnesota was hot and that we had to put out the fire, so we went right to work recapturing complete control of the game.

Starting from our 18 after the ensuing kickoff, we moved to the 32 on four plays and were faced with a big third down and seven yards to go. Frank Pitts took the ball on a flanker reverse and barely kicked up the first down as he was run out of bounds on our 39. A 15-yard penalty for roughing the passer moved the ball to Minnesota's 46 where Dawson passed to Otis Taylor in the flat, and Otis went all the way for the touchdown.

The pass itself covered only five yards out to the right, and Taylor was almost nailed at the 41. But he broke away from cornerback Earsell Mackbee, and then raced past Karl Kassulke, Minnesota's safety. It was truly a great individual effort typical of Otis.

149

Stenerud's extra point made it 23-7 and the scoring for the day was over at 13:38 of the third quarter.

Our defense could not have been better the remainder of the game as we picked off three interceptions and did not allow Minnesota to get closer than our 46-yard line.

It was a great victory, and made me extremely proud of our team. Football is a game of attitude. Ability alone will not win championships. Our players not only reached down and gave us 100 per cent of their true ability, but they also had the proper attitude. Each player made every personal sacrifice necessary for the success of the team. They were totally committed and completely involved in being champions.

We became the world champions of professional football on January 11, 1970, because we had 40 dedicated people playing with great spirit, discipline, unity, and determination; and because of the great effort and maturity shown by our squad, the Super Bowl victory will long live as my most memorable game as a pro coach.

Alex Webster

1969 NFL Game
New York 24, Minnesota 23

Alex Webster had only two years of experience as an assistant coach when he was tapped to bring the New York Giants out of a nine-game losing streak.

He did just that by winning his first game and finished the 1969 season with a 6–8 record. In 1970, he lifted the Giants to a 9–5 mark and just missed landing in the National Football Conference playoffs, losing to Los Angeles in the final game of the season.

Webster's performance during his second season earned him the Pro Coach of the Year award by the Washington Touchdown Club and the National Conference Coach of the Year designation by United Press International.

"Big Red" was graduated from North Carolina State in 1953. After being drafted by the Washington Redskins, he failed to make the team. He played two years with the Montreal Alouettes under the late Peahead Walker and was given another chance in the National Football League in 1955.

This time he made good with the Giants and became one of the team's and league's all-time greats as a running back. Webster played on one world's championship team—the 1956 Giants—and on six Eastern Division champions (1956, 1958, 1959, 1961, 1962 and 1963).

Webster still holds three Giant career records—most touchdowns rushing (39), most yardage rushing (4,805) and most rushing attempts (1,213).

It wasn't very difficult for me to select my most memorable game as a head coach. It was my very first game, played at Yankee Stadium in New York on September 21, 1969, and we upset a very tough Minnesota team, 24-23, with a touchdown in the final minute of play.

I had been named head coach only one week before this season opener, and I must admit that I was a bit scared about the whole thing. Here I was the head coach of one of the great franchises in pro football with only two years of experience as an assistant coach.

The team had lost nine games in a row: four at the end of the 1968 season and all five of our pre-season exhibitions that year. So being able to beat a power-house like Minnesota before a capacity hometown crowd will be a game that I will never forget.

That entire week had been an exciting one. It all started on a day off for me after we had played in Montreal the night before. I was home with my family when I received a phone call and was asked to come right down to the Giants' office. I thought that I had been fired or that something had gone wrong, but when I got there, Mr. Wellington Mara, the team's president, offered me the head coaching job. I was stunned. It was a big moment in my life; a real challenge for me, and I happily accepted.

The first thing I did was call my bride and tell her what had happened. She broke down and cried. Then I called all the assistant coaches and let them know the news and asked them to stay on. I wanted them to believe in me and take part in an organization which I felt we could rebuild.

When the squad assembled the next day, I had a long talk with them. I told them that I knew that football was a business as well as a great sport, but like everything else in life, the important thing was to have as much fun as possible and enjoy their job. Since I had been a player for 12 years myself, I knew how many of them lived. I told them that there was a time to relax, a time to take their families out and a time when they could have a cocktail, but I made it clear that there also was a certain cut-off date when you have to go to work and get ready for the next ball game.

I asked them to work twice as hard for me because I needed their help. I reminded them that it was useless to look over our shoulders, that everything was in our future. Nobody was going to help us, and we had to go out and make our own breaks. Strange things often happen during a game, and the ball is going to take funny bounces. In the past couple of years, the ball had bounced the wrong way for us, but I've always believed that if you don't get discouraged and if you work hard enough, the ball is eventually going to bounce towards you. But the important thing I told the squad was to remember that they had to make their own breaks.

During the next few days, I had individual talks with some of the players who, I thought, could really help us but were being bothered by certain problems. I told them that I didn't care what kind of trouble they were in and what their problems were, either personal or business-wise, but I wanted them to tell me about it.

I made it clear that I didn't want to hear about their problems from any source but them, and that they could depend upon me to try to help them in every way possible. I felt that a player who had problems off the field could not give 100 per cent on the field, and when you can't give 100 per cent, you aren't much good to your team.

We took a different approach to working with the players that week. Practice sessions were cut down, and I tried to get the squad to be more at ease. I made everybody responsible for certain things. It all seemed to help improve their morale.

The toughest thing I had to do that first week was to cut the squad down to 40 players, and this meant letting three players go. The first fellow I released was probably one of my closest friends, Jim Katcavage, but now I'm fortunate in having him on my staff as a defensive coach.

I put in long hours that first week because I had so much to learn. I turned over much of the Minnesota film to my defensive and offensive coaches. I put Norb Hecker completely in charge of the defense, and I stayed with the offense myself since I am basically an offensive player.

We had a good rundown on the Vikings. To me, they were one of the top defensive teams in pro football, and I felt that we would not be able to do much running against their great front four. We planned to pass as much as possible and concentrate on short passes against weak spots among their linebackers.

Long passes would be too risky against Minnesota's strong zone defense, and, of course, we were afraid that their front four's big rush wouldn't give Fran Tarkenton enough time to throw deep.

We wanted to run just enough to keep their defense honest and make our passing game work.

As far as the Minnesota offensive was concerned, we were more worried about their ground game since they had some fine runners. They didn't have a fancy-dan type offense. Minnesota liked to grind it out in small chunks, controlling the ball and beating you into the ground.

We looked at Gary Cuozzo almost as if he were a rookie since he had not been used much as a first string quarterback before. If we could stop Minnesota's running attack, we felt we could beat them.

We didn't plan to do much blitzing. We were going to use a lot of over-shifts and under-shifts. Nothing fancy—just enough confusion to shut down their ground game.

We expected very little blitzing against us. With a scrambler like Tarkenton, we love to have a team blitz us, but since Fran had played with Minnesota and they knew him well, there would be little or no blitzing by the Vikings.

I was nervous before the game started, but that's how it was when I was a player. And just like it was during my playing days, once the game started, I lost my nervousness.

Minnesota received the kickoff and was moving the ball too well for our comfort when Tommy Crutcher intercepted a Cuozzo pass intended for Dave Osborn on the Viking 47.

That seemed to give us a quick lift, and we took advantage of the break. On third and 11 from the Minnesota 24, Tarkenton could find no receiver open and was forced to run the ball himself. However, he failed to pick up the first down, and at that stage, we happily settled for a 25-yard field goal by Pete Gogolak.

Our 3-0 lead was short-lived. Clinton Jones took Gogolak's kickoff on his five-yard line and ran 71 yards to our 24 before Spider Lockhart, one of our best tacklers, made a great effort and prevented Jones from going all the way. It was a complete breakdown on the part of our defensive alignment on the kickoff, and you can't win ball games when your specialty teams fail you.

Osborn carried the ball four times in a row to our three-yard line, but our defense tightened up, and we were lucky to come out of it with Fred Cox's 11-yard field goal to tie the game.

Neither team could do much the rest of the first period, but the second quarter was less than two minutes old when Minnesota took the lead on a 47-yard touchdown pass from Cuozzo to John Henderson. Henderson had managed to get about five yards behind Scott Eaton, grabbed the ball on the 15 and easily made it into the end zone. There had been a breakdown in communications in our secondary with somebody missing his assignment. This was the sort of thing that had been beating us in previous games, and once again it looked like our own mistakes were going to prove disastrous.

The very next time that Minnesota got the ball they scored again, and it was 17-3 with almost nine minutes remaining in the half. This time Minnesota moved 71 yards in just four plays, with passing by Cuozzo, whom we had not expected to be very effective, eating up most of the yardage. First it was a 20-yard toss to Gene Washington, who grabbed the ball on his own 40 and ran an additional 30 yards to our 30-yard line. A holding penalty pushed them back to the 48, but on second and 28, we gambled on a blitz and failed.

We had thought that after the penalty they would be going to the air, and if we could break through and get to the passer before he could throw the ball, it would be a big break for us. It meant putting more pressure on our secondary which was covering man for man, and the strategy backfired. Washington got into the clear, Cuozzo threw to him on the 12, and Gene went in for the touchdown.

Trailing 17-3, I was afraid that the team was just going to fold up, roll over and play dead. I told the players to forget about their mistakes. I reminded them that Minnesota had been able to score two quick touchdowns against us and that we were capable of doing the same thing against them.

There's a lot of things that run through your mind in a situation like that. You're always trying to find ways to give the team a lift. There's not much you can do about your game plan. You finalized it on Thursday or Friday, and now it's just a question of each player carrying out his assignment and giving 100 per cent effort.

I was somewhat encouraged by the way the team moved the ball near the end of the half. We were able to get to Minnesota's 27-yard line, but Gogolak's field goal attempt was wide. Then, with time running out, we lost another chance by fumbling on their 35-yard line.

We came off the field trailing, 17-3, and the score just as easily could have been 35-3 at that point. I had no intention of changing our game plan. We would stay with the same offense and defense, and I knew that if we didn't quit, the ball would start bouncing our way.

I didn't criticize any individuals for their mistakes. A couple of bombs they completed hurt us, but there's no use harping on those mistakes. The player who was beaten knows all about his failure to cover properly so why get him more upset?

I told the squad that the Vikings were sitting in their dressing room and were very cocky at this stage because we were the New York Giants who had not won a game in our last nine starts and they had really handled us pretty easily this first half.

I said that if we went out there in the second half and took off after them with 100 per cent effort from every man, you never could tell but the ball could start bouncing our way.

That has always been my philosophy. You have to think "win" and believe in yourself in order to come out on top.

I made it clear that I wanted no quitters on my ball club, and I was going to find out in this second half which players were going all out for the team.

I warned them that anybody who would lay down would no longer be with us because, if we had to lose, I wanted to lose with fighters and not with quitters.

I took Tarkenton aside and told him that he was the leader and that he was the one who could get our offense going. If he kept his poise and kept everyone on their toes, I was sure that he could put it all together for us.

As we lined up to receive the second-half kickoff, I

had a strong feeling that we were going to pull this one out. Fuqua took Cox's kick on the seven-yard line and ran it back to our 31 from where we drove for a touchdown in just six plays.

Tarkenton passed to Hermann for five, and after Fredrickson failed to gain over left tackle, he took a screen pass from Fran and fought his way to the 42, barely making the first down. Another Tarkenton pass failed, and Fredrickson picked up four yards up the middle. Then, on third and six, Fran spotted Homer Jones open on the Minnesota 30 and hit him with a quick pass. Jones, a big, strong boy, broke away from Earsell Mackbee at the 30 and then managed to break another tackle on the 20 where Bobby Bryant had attempted to stop him. It was a 54-yard play with Jones lining up on the short side of the field and running a simple down and in pattern against their zone.

We were back in the ball game after 2:58 of the third period, but the Vikings had us in trouble after the ensuing kickoff.

Hitting us with the type of ball control game they loved, the Vikings ground it out against us from their 20 to our eight-yard line. Dave Osborn gained a yard, Bill Brown lost one and Cuozzo's pass to Osborn netted nothing as Brenner diagnosed the play perfectly. Once again we were happy when Minnesota was forced to settle for Cox's 17-yard field goal, but now I was worried about the way the Vikings were controlling the ball. They had used 15 plays in that drive, eating up more than six minutes of the clock.

160

Late in the third quarter, Tarkenton dropped back to pass and was decked so hard by Jim Marshall that he fumbled. Lonnie Warwick recovered for the Vikings on our 21, and once again, the burden was on our defense. Osborn and Brown alternated to give them a first down on our six-yard line, but our defense was great and on fourth and goal from our two, Cox booted a 10-yard field goal, making it 23-10 at 51 seconds of the fourth quarter.

There was some consolation in the way our defense was performing. On three occasions, Minnesota had first downs inside our 10-yard line, and each time they had been unable to get in for a touchdown.

Neither team could do much the next two times each had possession and there was 8:45 left in the game when we got our hands on the ball for the third time in the quarter. This time, we had good field position after a Minnesota punt of only 31 yards gave us the ball on our own 41.

Since we now needed two touchdowns to win and time was starting to run out, the Vikings figured that we had to go to the air. Tarkenton crossed them up with a great call for a draw, and Fredrickson went up the middle for 11. After a pass for Hermann was incomplete, Fran tried another draw, and this time Fredrickson went 19 yards to Minnesota's 30. It was another excellent call by Fran against the tremendous rush of Minnesota's front four. Of course, these are always brilliant maneuvers when you do everything right and the draw works. But let someone miss an assignment and it becomes a bum call.

With our running game so effective, Minnesota had to adjust its defense accordingly, and now we felt our chances for completing passes were much better. A toss to Jones was good for six yards, and Fredrickson picked up another first down with seven yards over tackle. Morrison gained two around left end, but a pass to Fredrickson in the right flat lost a yard. On third and nine from the 16, Hermann made a leaping catch on the two-yard line and broke away from Bobby Bryant and Wally Hilgenberg to score. It was a zig pattern in which Hermann took the defender in one direction and, when he got him running that way, cut sharply the opposite way. It was a perfectly executed play, with Hermann making a great move and Tarkenton throwing the ball to the right spot at the right time.

The touchdown came at 10:12 of the period, and we now trailed by only six points. We had the momentum, but it was up to the defense to get the ball for us.

On third and five from their own 25, Cuozzo completed a pass to Washington on the 36 for a first down, but Lockhart hit Washington with a jolting tackle causing him to fumble and Ralph Heck recovered for us. This was one of the biggest plays of the game by our defense. If we had not forced the fumble, Minnesota with its ball control game might have run out the clock.

However, with 2:58 left to play, we were given a big chance. Once again, with Minnesota expecting Tarkenton to pass, he called for a quick draw up the middle, and Fuqua picked up nine big yards. A holding penalty pushed us back to the 43, and a pass to Fredrickson in the flat was incomplete. On third and 17, with two minutes left, there's only one thing to do, and Minnesota was ready for the pass. Their front four was determined to nail Tarkenton, and Fran was immediately trapped in the pocket. But as he has done so many times, he somehow managed to scramble out of the pocket. In sheer desperation, he threw the ball some 50 yards in the air down field to a crowd that included two Giants and two Minnesota players. It seemed as though all four went up for the ball at the same time. Krause, the Viking free safety, tipped the ball but could not hold on to it. Butch Wilson, our reserve tight end who had just replaced the injured Freeman White, came across the middle and picked the ball out of the air.

It was a 33-yard gain, and a first down on the 10. It was a fluke play, but the ball was really bouncing our way for a change.

Fredrickson was held without gain around left end, but Tarkenton and Hermann teamed up on another perfectly executed pass play to tie the score with 59 seconds left in the game. Hermann made another of his great moves on a zig pattern, going down a few yards and then cutting in.

Gogolak's kick gave us a 24-23 lead, but those final seconds seemed like hours until the gun sounded.

The players picked me up and carried me off the field and I felt as though we had just won the world's championship.

I was happy not only for myself but for the players.

None of them quit in the second half. They stayed right in there, giving me that 100 per cent effort needed for a victory.

I had felt all along that the Giants were a better team than their record indicated, and I was sure that this win was a big step on their way to regaining their confidence.

The performance of our defensive unit was the best I have ever seen by the Giants, and we have had some great defensive teams in the past.

As for our offense, I can't say enough about the way Fredrickson and Tarkenton came through in the clutch. Tucker carried the ball 13 times for 77 yards against the mighty Minnesota front four, and his blocking was superb.

Tucker's ability to run against Minnesota helped make our passing game work, and Fran was just magnificent with 18 completions for three touchdowns and 228 yards.

I hope to see the Giants win the Super Bowl one day soon, but when we do, I don't think that I will be any happier than I was after my very first game as a head coach.

Don McCafferty

1970 NFL Game
Baltimore 21, Chicago 20

Don McCafferty spent a long apprentice-ship as an assistant coach, and in 1970, when a head coaching position finally beck-oned, the six-foot-five former Ohio State tackle was ready for the challenge.

In his very first season as top man with the Baltimore Colts, he guided the team to pro football's world's championship by defeating Dallas on a field goal in the closing seconds of Super Bowl V.

Don had spent 10 years as an assistant at Kent State University and 11 years as an aide to Weeb Ewbank and Don Shula at Bal-timore before the No. 1 spot became his.

He played tackle at Ohio State under the late Francis Schmidt and Paul Brown and per-formed in both the 1945 and 1946 College All Star games in Chicago.

McCafferty was signed by the New York Giants, who shifted him to end during the 1946 season, but was released after the 1947 exhibition schedule was completed. He landed with the Giants' farm team in Jersey City for the rest of the season and then tried his hand as a high school teacher in Cleveland for six months before he had the chance to coach at Kent State.

In 1956, when Ewbank offered him a job at Baltimore, McCafferty turned it down, preferring the security at Kent State, but two years later, when Weeb again asked him to join the Colts' staff, Don accepted. Under Ewbank, McCafferty was an end coach and became offensive co-ordinator when Shula became the Baltimore head coach.

You win the world's professional football championship the very first year that you are a head coach so it would almost seem natural to select the win over Dallas in the Super Bowl as your most memorable game.

I did give considerable thought to Super Bowl V, since it was a fantastic game and a great victory for us, but in the long run, I felt that Baltimore's 21-20 triumph over the Chicago Bears on November 29, 1970, in Baltimore is the game that stands foremost in my memories.

If we had not won that game, we probably would never have been in the Super Bowl in the first place.

Two weeks before the game with the Bears, we wound up in a tie with Buffalo when we should have beaten them, and just one week later, we had lost 34-17 to the Miami Dolphins, a team we had clobbered, 35-0, in our first meeting.

It seemed like we were going downhill, and we realized that a loss to Chicago could mean the last straw for us.

Doomsday appeared to be setting in as we trailed the Bears, 17-0, after only seven minutes in the first quarter, but instead of completely collapsing, our ball club fought back with all the courage you would expect from a team of championship calibre.

This was a tough Chicago Bears team we were playing, even though their win-loss record wasn't very impressive. The Bears are always tough and seem to give Baltimore a great deal of trouble everytime we play them.

They may not beat you as far as the score is concerned, but they whip you physically and soften you up for your next opponent. I'm always happy when a game against the Bears is over and our casualty list isn't too bad.

When I first met with our squad on the Tuesday before the Chicago game, I chewed them out for the sloppy way they had played against Miami. That has always been one of the most distasteful things for me to do as a coach. I wish that it could be avoided, but you can't mince words with your players. If they make mistakes, if they loaf or shirk their duties, you have to tell it to them the way it is.

You don't have to holler and scream at the players. I learned that was unnecessary during the years I played under Paul Brown at Ohio State. You can be just as effective in getting across your message without raising your voice.

The game against Miami had been a comedy of errors. We had dropped pass after pass. We fumbled a punt. We had allowed them to score much too easily on long plays, so I felt it necessary to let them know just how poorly they had performed.

The lecture didn't last long, and I told them to forget about last week and start preparing for the Bears game.

Actually, our coaching staff had started preparation for the Bears on Monday. While the players had the day off to rest up, I met with the coaches to review the films of the Miami game. All coaches made notations about the performances of the players.

Then, we took a look at the films we had received of the Bears' games. We were worried about Chicago's defense. When you play against a team with a linebacker as great as Dick Butkus, you have your work cut out for you. Butkus was the key to the Bears' defense, and you have to plan on keeping your offensive plays as far away from him as possible.

On Tuesday, after our squad meeting, everyone took a look at the films of the Miami game. Then, the players broke into groups, and the coaches made constructive criticisms of the players' performances. This was followed by a short workout, mainly to get the players loosened up.

After a brief rest, the squad watched films of the

Bears' games, and we checked our scouting reports about them. The day ended for the players with a discussion of our offensive and defensive plans for the game.

However, the day's work was not over for the coaches. We continued to work on our plans until 9:30 p.m. when we finally broke for dinner.

Wednesday was our offensive day. Both morning and afternoon sessions were devoted to testing our running and passing plays against the Chicago defense and trying to find the most effective.

The Bears had altered their defense in 1970 and were using a wide variety of defenses, including some unusual fronts, so we were experimenting against the different type coverage they had been using.

Thursday was our defensive day, and we had decided to make several changes in our starting lineup after reviewing the films of the Miami game. We moved Jimmy Duncan to right cornerback, put Ray May at left linebacker and decided to give Roy Hilton another shot at right end.

We spent that day concentrating on Chicago's short yardage running plays, and we were satisfied that we could contain their offense.

Friday was our combination day when we worked with both our offensive and defensive units. After a session of pass offense, pass defense, running offense, and defense against runs, we went into our two-minute drill which always seems to be the fun part of practice for the players.

Our week of practice ended on Saturday, which is

our kicking day. We look at films showing both our and Chicago's kickoffs, kickoff returns, punts and field goal tries. Then, we go over exactly what we want to do on these plays.

The entire squad, along with the coaches, went to a motel in the evening, and after a snack at 9:30, the players were in their rooms for an 11 o'clock bed check.

The worst part of any week during the football season is the day of the game. It's rough on the players and coaches waiting around for the game to start. Of course, the players get taped and dressed and warm up for part of the time. But there always seems to be too much time to kill before the kick-off.

We reviewed some of the things we did during the past week, but there was no pep talk as such. We had been building up for this all week, and I thought we were ready for the Bears. Just before we took the field, Bob Vogel led the squad in prayer which is traditional before and after all our games.

We won the toss, and Jimmy Duncan ran the kickoff from the end zone back to our 28-yard line. Passes by John Unitas to Norm Bulaich and Eddie Hinton were dropped on the first two plays, and it looked like this was going to be Miami all over again. On third and 10, John passed again, and this time Ross Brupbacker, who was being used as a fourth linebacker by the Bears, intercepted on our 41-yard line and ran the ball back to the 36.

The Bears picked up 16 yards on two plays and

170

had a first down on our 20. Jack Concannon passed to George Farmer, who made the catch at the goal line for the touchdown.

On that play, Duncan, our right cornerback, was late adjusting to an audible defensive call. He had been expecting some inside help, and when he didn't get it, Farmer was left open and made an easy reception.

Mac Percival booted the extra point and after only 2:11 of the first period, we were behind, 7-0, and in the unenviable position of having to play catch-up football so early in the game.

Starting from our own 20 after the kickoff Jerry Hill gained five yards over right tackle but then dropped a pass from Unitas at the line of scrimmage. On third and five, Ed O'Bradovich deflected a Unitas pass intended for Hill on an outlet valve, and George Seals was in the right spot at the right time to pick it off on our 22. Actually, Seals was still on the line of scrimmage because our offensive linemen had kept him from making a good rush.

The Bears could gain only one yard on three plays and settled for a 28-yard field goal by Percival. It was now 10-0, and only 3:40 had been played in the game.

On the very first play after the next kickoff, Unitas attempted a pass to Tom Mitchell, but Dick Daniels, Chicago's right safety, intercepted at our 43 and raced back to the 27.

It was hard to believe. Unitas had attempted six passes. Three were dropped and three were intercepted. It looked like we were really falling apart.

Concannon's pass to Dick Gordon in the end zone was overthrown, but Jerry Logan, our left safety, was charged with pass interference, placing the ball on the one-yard line. Everything was going against us.

After a running play failed, Concannon tossed to tight end Rich Coady in the end zone for the touchdown. Percival converted, and it was 17-0 at exactly seven minutes of the first period.

I just could not believe that our team had slipped so badly. We had won seven out of our first eight games before being tied by Buffalo and beaten by Miami the last two weeks. The slump of the last two weeks was continuing, and our hopes for a championship were rapidly disappearing.

When you are coaching on the sidelines, you hear the crowd and the noises, but you rarely hear anything an individual in the stands says. This day, I heard only too clearly one fan yell: "Hey, McCafferty! What do you think of your defensive changes now?"

Well, our being behind, 17-0, had nothing to do with our defense. The offense had turned the ball over three times in our own territory, and we were lucky it wasn't 21-0.

It all happened so fast that I didn't even give any thought of taking Unitas out of there. Even if I had thought about it, I probably would have stayed with him. You know that a passer as great as Unitas is going to snap out of it sooner or later, and when you have to play catch-up football, I guess I'd rather go with John than anyone else.

We managed to get through the next series of plays without an interception, and when we kicked to the Bears' 27-yard line, it was the first time that they were starting from their own territory.

They didn't stay there very long as Don Shy broke over the middle, raced up the left side for a 45-yard gain before Charlie Stukes, our left cornerback, tackled him on our 16 to prevent another touchdown.

Following an incompleted pass to Coady, Concannon tried to go to the air again, but Mike Curtis busted through to nail him for an eight-yard loss. Concannon passed to Farmer on the eight, but the Bears had an ineligible player downfield and were penalized back to the 39.

That penalty was the first favorable break we received, and relieved us of some of the pressure. The Bears tried to surprise us with a draw on third and 32, but we were ready and it was good for only a yard. Percival came in to attempt a field goal from the 45, but it was wide and we took over on our 20.

We seemed to come alive at this point. Unitas hit on three passes, and we had a first down on the Bears' 44 as the first period ended.

At long last, we were in Bear territory. A pass to Hinton was almost intercepted by Chicago's right cornerback Joe Taylor, but Unitas came right back on a screen pass to Mitchell, our tight end, who stayed in his block and then slipped out into the flat.

That gave us a first down on the 28, and Unitas called a beautiful trap pass play that worked to perfection and put the ball on the one. This play gave every indication of being a running play. Sam Havrilak, the running back, came out of the backfield and headed towards the linebacker as if to block him.

The guard pulled as he would on a running play, and when the linebacker decided to rush in, Havrilak moved out. Unitas was under a heavy rush but tossed the ball quickly to Sam, who almost made it all the way.

Hill hit left guard for the touchdown from the one, and Jim O'Brien's kick cut the Bears' lead to 17-7 at 57 seconds of the second period.

The game settled down to a defensive battle until late in the quarter when Ron Gardin, our rookie safety, returned a punt to the Bears' 45. A pass and then a running play gave us a first down on the 30. On third and 8 from the 28, John hit Havrilak on a screen pass which was just good enough for a first down on the 20.

Hill tried the middle for no gain, and a pass to Hinton was incomplete. On third and 10, Unitas could not find anyone open downfield far enough for the first down, and he had to throw to Mitchell as an outlet. Mitchell could gain only seven yards, leaving us three yards short of a first down.

Unitas called time out and came to the sideline to discuss the situation with me. It was a major decision. There was only a minute left to play in the half. Do you go for the sure three points with a field goal or do you take the gamble and try for the touchdown? If you fail to get the touchdown, you're in serious trouble, but if you make the touchdown, you can leave the field trailing only 17-14 and with momentum to carry you through to victory in the second half.

I decided that with a clutch quarterback like Unitas the gamble would not be too great, so I told John to call for a 40 pass. On this play, we have two receivers, Hinton and Roy Jefferson, who are No. 1 targets, depending upon what the defense shows. Unitas passed to Hinton, who made a great one-handed grab just before stepping out-of-bounds on the seven-yard line for the first down.

It's funny what some people will read into a game. After it was all over, there was talk that Unitas decided to throw to Hinton because Eddie had previously dropped two passes, and it would help him regain his confidence.

Hell, we weren't interested in anything but getting the first down. When the two teams lined up, I knew that Unitas was going to throw to Hinton because the man on Jefferson was right up on him while the man on the left covering Hinton was off a bit.

On the top of the next page is a diagram of that play.

On the next play, Unitas and Jefferson teamed up on another perfectly executed play for the touchdown. This was a quick take-off play which we normally use for a bomb, but in this case, Jefferson made a quick move and ran to the corner of the end zone

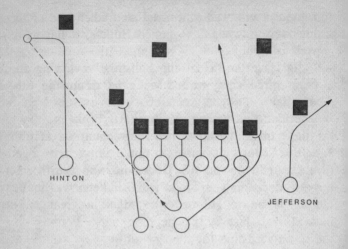

HINTON

JEFFERSON

while Unitas took a couple of steps back and laid the ball out there.

On the bottom of the next page is a diagram of the touchdown play.

Naturally, we felt a bit happier being behind only 17-14 at the half after having fallen behind 17-0 in the first seven minutes.

Unitas was passing better after his horrible start, but our running game still was quite bad. We had been able to gain only 38 yards rushing on 14 carries. On the other hand, Unitas, after missing on his first six passes, was 14 out of 25 for 142 yards.

The Bears were using a three-man line with four linebackers, and it was confusing us. The extra linebacker was making the big difference as far as our running game was concerned, and when one of those linebackers is a fellow named Butkus, it has to hurt you.

We spent much of the half-time reviewing those plays which had worked well and discussing others which we thought could be better exploited in the second half.

The third quarter turned into a punting duel with neither team being able to put a long drive together. Late in the period, Unitas had his fourth interception of the day, but at least this one was in Bear territory, and coupled with a clipping penalty, set them back to their 11.

Chicago moved to our 41 where on fourth and two, Percival came in for a 48-yard field-goal try. Percival faked the kick and caught us by surprise by

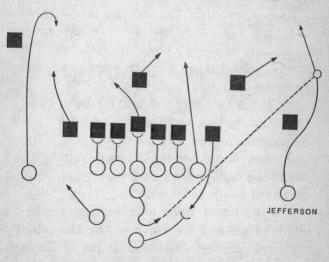

JEFFERSON

going downfield himself and catching a pass from Concannon. Duncan saved a touchdown by nailing Percival on the 23.

Our defensive backs had been completely fooled. Normally, on a long field-goal attempt, they will watch the ends or the fullback in protecting against a fake, but in this case, it was the kicker who ran out for the pass, and nobody covered him.

Our defense held after that, and the Bears were forced to settle for a 27-yard field goal by Percival, giving them a 20-17 lead at 3:19 of the fourth period.

We were in trouble once again soon after the kickoff when Unitas had his fifth pass of the day intercepted. John was supposed to throw to Bulaich on a halfback option play, but Norm was covered and John whipped the ball to Tom Nowatzke, who was coming out of the backfield on the opposite side. Butkus, who was everywhere you looked that afternoon, leaped high and made a great one-handed interception on our 43.

Our defense took over and held the Bears to seven yards on three plays, and Percival missed a 43-yard field-goal attempt.

The clock was becoming a factor. Getting close enough for a field goal wasn't good enough. We had to go all the way.

There were only about five minutes remaining when we took over on our own 24 after Gardin made a fair catch of a punt. Unitas passed 22 yards to John Mackey and then hit John on a 54-yard scoring play.

Mackey was a decoy on this play, with Jimmy Orr the primary target on an individual outside pattern. Unitas saw that they were using a zone on Orr and since the pattern he was running wasn't good against zone coverage, John looked for his secondary receiver, Jefferson, on the opposite side. But they had a zone there, too.

John glanced down the middle, and there was Mackey all by himself. Unitas ducked away from a

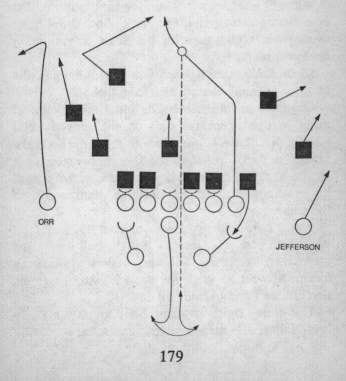

Chicago lineman and zipped the ball to Mackey, who made an easy catch on the 30, put a move on Gary Lyle, the free safety, at the 14 and went into the end zone standing up.

Later on, we found out that the Bears had messed up their coverage on the play. An audible had been called to switch from the zone, but someone failed to hear the change, and Mackey was allowed to get free. It was a lucky break for us, but we deserved a good one after all the bad luck we had earlier in the game.

When O'Brien, our rookie place-kicker, booted the tie-breaking extra point, the clock showed 3:47 left to play—plenty of time for the Bears to get within field goal range.

Once again, our defense was great, holding the Bears and forcing them to kick from their 13.

Only two minutes remained, and I told Unitas to make sure he kept the ball on the ground. You usually don't have to worry about a quarterback like Unitas in a spot like that, but I kept remembering a similar situation earlier that year when we were leading Boston, 7-6, with about three minutes left in the game.

It was third and two from our own 45, and John decided to pass. The seconds that the ball was in the air seemed like hours, but when Jefferson made the catch and went 55 yards for a touchdown, it was the first chance I had to smile all day.

This time, Unitas wasn't about to give me any heart failure. He stayed on the ground and actually got us close enough for a shot at a field goal, but O'Brien's boot from the 44 rolled dead on the 10.

The Bears still had one more chance, but four plays gained only one yard, and victory was ours.

However, for a while it looked like we might have won the battle but lost the war. Our casualty list, always high after a Bears game, was worse than usual. Jim Bailey, our defensive tackle, was lost for the season. Fred Miller, our other defensive tackle, was injured, along with three offensive guards, Glenn Ressler, John Williams and Cornelius Johnson; offensive tackle Bob Vogel; defensive end Bubba Smith and halfback Norm Bulaich.

Not one player complained about the physical beating they had taken from the Bears. They were pleased—and justly so—about their courageous comeback which eventually carried Baltimore into the Super Bowl.

Jack Fleischer has a total of twenty-five years of experience as sports writer, broadcaster, columnist, and editor, and during that time has personally interviewed almost every major figure in the sports world, including the professional football coaches whose stories are included in this book. During the 1960 Presidential campaign he was News Director for Lyndon B. Johnson at his Washington headquarters, and in 1961-62 he was the Executive Director of the Democratic Senatorial Campaign Committee. He is presently a public relations consultant in Washington, D.C., where he makes his home.